The Apple Cookbook

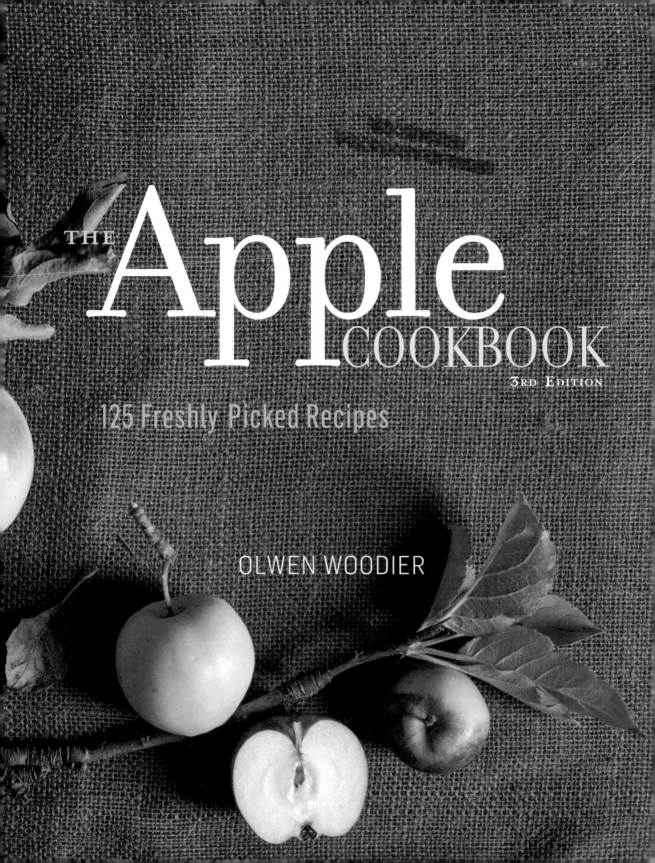

The Apple COOKBOOK

3RD EDITION

125 Freshly Picked Recipes

OLWEN WOODIER

The mission of Storey Publishing is to serve our customers by
publishing practical information that encourages
personal independence in harmony with the environment.

Edited by Margaret Sutherland, Sally Patterson, and Dianne M. Cutillo

Art direction and design by Mary Winkelman Velgos

Text production by Jennifer Jepson Smith

Indexed by Christine R. Lindemer, Boston Road Communications

Cover photography by © Leigh Beisch Photography, with food stylist Robyn Valarik, front cover (all
    but bottom left), back cover (left); © Sylvia Fountaine, front cover (bottom left); © Stacey Cramp
    Photography, with food stylist Vanessa Seder, back cover (right), inside cover (front and back)
Interior photography by © Leigh Beisch Photography, with food stylist Robyn Valarik, 37, 43, 47, 55,
    61, 69, 79, 91, 95, 109, 115, 123, 131, 135, 141, 145, 149, 167, 171, 175, 179, 183, 191; Mars Vilaubi, 220
    (bottom), 221, 222, 223, 224, 225, 227, 228, 229, 230; © Stacey Cramp Photography, with food
    stylist Vanessa Seder, 1, 2–3, 5, 6–7, 8, 9, 11, 14, 15, 16, 20–21, 22, 24, 28, 30, 35, 38, 50–51, 53, 57,
    64, 66–67, 75, 80, 86, 93, 98, 99, 100–101, 103, 111, 124, 125, 132–133, 138, 147, 151, 153, 173, 184,
    189, 198, 200, 205, 206, 207, 210, 217, 218–219, 220 (top), 232

Storey Publishing
210 MASS MoCA Way
North Adams, MA 01247
www.storey.com

Printed in the United States by Versa Press
10 9 8 7 6 5 4 3 2 1

LIBRARY OF CONGRESS CATALOGING-IN-PUBLICATION DATA
Woodier, Olwen, 1942–
  The apple cookbook / Olwen Woodier. — Third edition.
    pages cm
  Includes index.
  ISBN 978-1-61212-518-3 (pbk. : alk. paper)
  ISBN 978-1-61212-519-0 (ebook) 1. Cooking (Apples) I. Title.
TX813.A6W657 2015
641.6′411—dc23
                      2015000559

Contents

CHAPTER 1: Introduction to Apples   6

CHAPTER 2: Apple Breakfasts & Breads   20

CHAPTER 3: Apple Drinks & Snacks   50

CHAPTER 4: Apple Salads & Sides   66

CHAPTER 5: Apples Make the Meal   100

CHAPTER 6: Apple Desserts   132

CHAPTER 7: Preserving the Apple Harvest   205

CHAPTER 8: Meet the Apples: Apple Varieties   219

Appendixes   232

Acknowledgments   234

Index   235

Introduction
to Apples

M AN HAS BEEN MUNCHING ON APPLES FOR about 750,000 years, ever since the food gatherers of early Paleolithic times discovered sour, wild crab apples growing in the forests in Kazakhstan, in central Asia. Botanists now believe that this region holds the key to the genetic origins of the apples we enjoy today.

When U.S. botanists visited Kazakhstan in 1989, they found large stands of ancient apple trees — trees that were 300 years old, 50 feet tall, and bearing large, red apples. These trees of *Malus sieversii*, the wild species now believed to be the parent of all domesticated apples, were discovered in 1929 by Russian botanist Nikolai I. Vavilov.

Unfortunately, Vavilov's work in genetics led to his imprisonment during the Stalin era. He died in prison in 1943. His wonderful discovery was finally announced to the rest of the world by a former student and coworker of Vavilov's, who, at the age of 80, felt the need to pass along the knowledge before it was too late to save the forests of ancient apple trees.

Apples on the Move

The carbonized remains of apples unearthed in Asia Minor indicate that Neolithic farmers were cultivating apples around 8,000 years ago. Later, apples were carried as transportable food by migrating cultures. It is speculated that somewhere along the way *M. sieversii* hybridized with *M. orientalis* and *M. sylvestris*, two wild species producing small and very sour green apples.

There is recorded evidence from 1300 BCE of apple orchards being planted by the Egyptians along the Nile Delta. The Greeks learned grafting techniques around 800 BCE, and by 200 BCE the Romans were planting apple orchards in Britain.

Apples Settle in America

Colonists arriving in America found only four varieties of wild crab apples. However, the French, Dutch, German, and English all brought seeds from their homelands, and it wasn't long before apple trees were growing outside their rustic dwellings. The English colonists were the first to bring apple tree scions (shoots) to North America.

The first American orchard was planted in Boston in 1625 by William Blaxton, an English preacher. A few years later, orchards were established in the same area by John Winthrop and John Endicott, governors of the Bay Colony settlement.

In 1647, Peter Stuyvesant, governor of New Amsterdam (now New York), planted the first Dutch apple trees on his farm, the Bouwerie. The first commercial orchard was planted in Flushing, New York, in 1730.

Thousands of varieties of apple trees evolved during the eighteenth and nineteenth centuries when colonial farmers decided to plant apple seeds instead of acquiring young tree scions arriving from England and continental Europe. As the colonists moved from the Atlantic coast westward, they planted apple seeds along the way.

Favorably influenced by moderately cold winters, the colonists' apple crops flourished in the northern regions. Most apple tree varieties require from 1,000 to 1,500 hours of chilly temperatures before they will begin blossom growth in the spring. And the apples, just like autumn leaves, need the perfect marriage of temperatures — the warm, sunny days and cool nights that occur in September and October — to show off their best qualities.

America's Favorite Homegrown Fruit

Cultivated throughout the United States, apples are grown for commercial production in 36 states. The main apple-growing regions are Washington, New York, Michigan, Pennsylvania, California, and Virginia. These six states produce most of the country's annual apple crop, which totaled 259,248 million bushels in 2013. About one-third of the annual U.S. apple crop is processed into juice and canned, frozen, and dehydrated products. The average American eats 50.4 pounds of apples a year. It's not only their year-round availability that makes apples so desirable in the United States; there are a host of other reasons why America loves apples:

* They are delicious, versatile, and easily portable.
* They are nutritious, providing satisfying bulk and few calories. (See page 72 for information on nutritional values.)
* They are 85 to 95 percent water, so if you put one into your pocket or lunch box, you can quench your thirst whenever the need arises.
* Their acid content acts as a natural mouth freshener, which makes apples a perfect ending to a meal.
* They are believed to have many other healthful properties. (See page 64 for further information.)

Apple Allure

When Eve was tempted by the serpent in the Garden of Eden to go against God's wishes and to take what was forbidden "of the fruit of the tree which is in the middle of the garden," she "saw that the tree was good for food, and that it was pleasant to the eyes, and a tree to be

THE ORIGIN OF THE APPLE

ON DISCOVERING THE ANCIENT WILD APPLE GROVES in central Asia, Nikolai Vavilov rejoiced:

"All around the city one could see a vast expanse of wild apples covering the foothills. One could see with his own eyes that this beautiful site was the origin of the cultivated apple."

desired to make one wise." No doubt she was also quite taken by the shape, color, and smell of this "fruit of the gods."

Imagine yourself picking up an apple for the very first time. Turn it around in your hand. If it's one of the russet apples, it will feel rough and dry, not at all like a red-on-yellow Empire with its satiny smooth and tender skin. Hold it to your nose and breathe deeply. The smooth-skinned Empire will have a delicate smell that is difficult to detect beneath its smooth and slightly oily skin. The rough skin of a ripe russet, on the other hand, will exude a tantalizing fragrance.

Most of the perfume cells are concentrated in the skin of an apple. As the apple ripens, the cells give off a stronger aroma. That is why applesauce is most flavorful when made from apples with the skin left on and the best cider is made from the aromatic, tough-skinned russets.

Rosy pink applesauce gets its color from the flesh, not from the skin — unless the skin has been puréed with the flesh to become an integral part of the sauce. The pigments trapped in the skin cells are not released during cooking, crushing, or pressing because those color cells are impossible to break.

Apple trees not only have taken the fancy of gods and mortals, they attract more than 30 species of birds and a variety of four-legged animals. There are birds that love to nest in the spreading branches. Many birds and beasts feast on the buds, bark, and leaves. The ripe, fallen apples are favored by porcupines, skunks, fox, and deer. Opossums, raccoons, and bears all climb the limbs to get at apple-laden branches.

Popular Orchard Varieties

Although hundreds of varieties of apples are grown in the United States, only 20 or so best sellers are cultivated in the major commercial orchards. Most commercial apples are chosen not for their wonderful taste but for their bountiful harvest; their suitability to mass planting, shipping, and long storage; and their resistance to diseases. Breeders, however, are constantly working to produce new hybrids that are sweet-tart with crisp and juicy flesh and are as wonderful for eating out of hand as they are for cooking. And, of course, the trees should retain all the qualities that make them a viable commercial enterprise.

Apples in Season

The orchards are invaded by armies of apple pickers as early as July, but it is not until the cooler temperatures of September have touched this "fruit of immortality," as it was once called, that an apple takes on those crisp and crunchy qualities so important to orchardists and apple lovers. It is in autumn that a bite into a fresh-picked apple becomes a memorable experience; the apple spurts juice that is honey-sweet and yet also spicily tart, and the flesh is so fragrantly mellow.

After December, these fall beauties come to us from controlled storage — somewhere between 32 and 36°F. This controlled atmosphere helps maintain the crisp qualities of the fall-harvested apples for several months. Today, shoppers find that a reasonable selection of apples is available well after the last of the fresh harvest disappears into cold storage. From January through June, most of us can find such good keepers as Pink Lady

(Cripps Pink), Braeburn, Fuji, Gala, Golden Delicious, Granny Smith, Idared, McIntosh, Red Delicious, and Rome Beauty. In fact, Gala, Granny Smith, Golden Delicious, and Red Delicious are now available to us year-round from different hemispheres.

Detailed descriptions of apple varieties can be found in chapter 8.

Apple Breeding

The decline in the selection of apple varieties can be traced to the end of the nineteenth century and the advent of commercial orchards. After World War II, the decline was hastened by the horticultural practice of mass planting only a few reliable varieties that met certain requirements, such as the ability to produce heavy crops, resist diseases, endure long-distance transportation, and last in long-term cold storage. Smooth, evenly colored skin and pleasing shape also factored into the equation. Other varieties were chosen because they were the best candidates for large-scale production of juice, sauce, and pie filling. While these qualities tip the scales in favor of popularity with commercial growers, they narrow

the choice of varieties available to consumers, especially those who shop primarily in supermarkets.

Fortunately, apple breeders are always developing new varieties that have great growing qualities and taste delicious. Breeders develop new varieties by hybridizing (crossbreeding) two proven varieties.

The Lure of the New Hybrids

During the past few decades, North America has witnessed an influx of new varieties. Some, such as Braeburn, Gala, Jazz, and Pink Lady, started out as imports from Australia and New Zealand. However, because they have many desirable qualities that appeal to both growers and consumers, they have been mass planted throughout the United States and many countries worldwide. Today, these newcomers are in full production in U.S. orchards.

While pomologists (apple breeders) are concerned primarily with developing hybrid varieties that are resistant to the major apple diseases (scab, fire blight, mildew, and cedar apple rust), quality attributes are also stressed.

A number of modern-day apple varieties are endowed with sweet-tart, juicy, crisp flesh. For example, Honeycrisp, a cross between Macoun and Honeygold developed at the University of Minnesota in 1960, has aromatic, honey-sweet, crisp flesh that maintains its outstanding texture and flavor during long-term storage. Jonagold, a cross between Jonathan and Golden Delicious, is also a high-ranking apple in U.S. taste tests. And the Pink Lady apple from Australia (where it was developed as Cripps Pink) has become a raving success in the United States and Europe. A cross of Golden Delicious and Lady Williams, this crisp, more-sweet-than-tart apple has become so incredibly popular that it has its own U.K. website.

The new apple varieties Lady Alice, Piñata, Autumn Crisp, SweeTango, and Zestar! are reaching the market in limited quantities but are being picked up by consumers with great enthusiasm.

LADY ALICE. A chance seedling found in 1978 on a farm in Gleed, Washington, this medium-size round apple has tender skin flushed with pink and red over a yellow-orange background. The creamy, dense flesh is sweet-tart delicious and slow to brown, making it a good choice for salads, fruit trays, and eating out of hand. It is also a good all-purpose apple available out of long-term storage. Introduced to the consumer market in 2008, the Lady Alice apple is named in memory of Alice Zirkle, the cofounder of Rainier Fruit Company, the exclusive supplier of this incredible dessert apple. The Rainier Fruit Company has been growing fruit in the Northwest for over 100 years and is one of the largest growers of fresh apples, pears, cherries, and blueberries in the United States.

PIÑATA. German breeders successfully crossed Golden Delicious, Cox's Orange Pippin, and Duchess of Oldenburg in the 1970s. When the hybrid apple was released in Europe in 1986, it was marketed under the names Pinova and Sonata. The rights to grow and market the Pinova cultivar in the United States were acquired by the Stemilt Growers in Washington State. Choosing a name to represent both Pinova and Sonata, they trademarked their apple as Piñata.

This large, orange-yellow apple is heavily flushed with red. The white flesh is crisp, juicy, and sweet-tart flavorful. Piñata is a superb all-purpose apple and does well in long-term storage.

AUTUMN CRISP. This is the 63rd apple released from the breeding program at the Cornell University Research Station in Geneva, New York. A cross between Golden Delicious and Monroe apples, Autumn Crisp has a higher vitamin C content than many other varieties. Its skin shows a yellow background blushed with red. The crisp, juicy white flesh is enticingly sweet-tart, a flavorful balance of sugar and acid that makes it a good all-purpose apple. Because the white flesh is slow to brown, it is a perfect candidate for salads and fruit plates and a delight to eat out of hand. It is available only in September through December.

SWEETANGO. Introduced in 2009, this apple is the offspring of the Minneiska cultivar developed by apple breeders at the University of Minnesota by crossing Honeycrisp and Zestar!. Like Zestar!, SweeTango is a registered trademark of the university and grown only as a "managed variety." Growers must be licensed members of the Next Big Thing Cooperative and follow strict growing, harvesting, and shipping methods. So far, SweeTango is grown in Minnesota, Michigan, Washington, New York, and other northern states.

Harvested in late August and early September, SweeTango is available only for a few months through fall. However, the intensely crisp and crunchy flesh with sweet-tart spicy notes holds up longer under refrigeration. As with its parentage, the skin color of this apple has a yellow background deeply blushed with red. Already becoming a sought-after favorite, it is superbly delicious for eating fresh and can also be used for baking and cooking.

ZESTAR! Developed by University of Minnesota research scientists to withstand the harshest northern winters, Zestar!, the trademarked name of the patented Minnewashta cultivar, was introduced to consumers in 1999. Under Minnesota growing conditions, Zestar! apples ripen in late August to early September. However, unlike most early-season apples, they retain a crisp crunch to their zesty sweet-tart flesh for two months under refrigeration. This is a medium-size round apple with a creamy yellow background that is heavily blushed with rosy red.

The Lore of the Heirloom

One of the most promising trends in our ultramodern times is the return of interest in heirlooms, and particularly in those wonderful older varieties that got lost in the effort of mass production and distribution. (For information on specific heirloom varieties, see Hardy Heirloom Apple Varieties, page 226.)

More than 2,500 varieties of apples are grown at the New York State Agricultural Experiment Station in Geneva. One of the oldest agricultural research stations in the country, it is also the location for the U.S. Department of Agriculture's Plant Genetic Resources Unit, which houses the national apple collection. The apple varieties range from historical varieties that originated in central Asia, to experimental hybrids from heirlooms that were brought as seeds, cuttings, or trees to America by European and English settlers, to the antique apples of North America that were grown from seeds in the eighteenth century.

Many of these heirloom or antique apples rank among the best varieties for eating out of hand and for making the most flavorful pies, applesauce, and apple juice. However, because of their unreliable yields, susceptibility to diseases, and misshapen fruits, few old varieties are grown in large commercial orchards.

In an effort to save important heirlooms that may contain unique genes, researchers at the Plant Genetic Resources Unit are always on the lookout for new genetic material. The reason has less to do with the fact that many of the heirlooms produce aromatic, intensely flavorful apples than with the fact that they

represent genetic diversity. The key to safe-guarding against the loss of genetic diversity is to rescue germplasm, the genetic material contained in the seeds.

Seeds collected in central Asia and planted in Geneva are now bearing fruits, ranging in color, form, and shape from purple and cherrylike to yellow, conical, and of commercial size. The diversity of the wild and heirloom varieties growing at the Plant Genetic Resources Unit provides researchers with the opportunity to develop new hybrids and cultivars that will be disease and pest resistant, winter hardy, vigorous, and highly productive, and will bear apples that are flavorful and firm.

Working with Heirlooms

While there is interest among apple growers in planting historical varieties on a commercial level, the economics discourage large-scale production. Even though heirloom varieties are available as dwarf and semidwarf trees, which bear quicker and more abundantly than their large, spreading ancestors, they still take longer to bear fruit than the apple varieties favored by large commercial orchards.

Heirloom varieties are grown by a limited number of farms, such as Breezy Hill Orchard (profiled on page 199) in the Hudson Valley, New York, and Distillery Lane Ciderworks in Jefferson, Maryland (profiled on page 117). To buy heirloom varieties from these orchards, and from other antique-apple growers around the United States, you must contact the orchards directly or buy locally from specialty stores and farmers' markets. You'll find farmers' markets in major towns and big cities.

Cornell University's Apple-Breeding Program

Cornell's New York State Agricultural Experiment Station in Geneva is the major apple-breeding station in the United States. It was founded in 1880 to safeguard New York's production of fruits and vegetables, develop new crops, improve food safety for consumers, and promote economically sustainable farming solutions. For more than 125 years, the station has been developing cutting-edge technologies essential to feeding the world and working to serve millions of consumers, agricultural producers, food businesses, and farm families throughout New York State. It is also, however, a state-of-the art research resource for homeowners, farmers, and researchers all over the world.

Also located at the New York State Agricultural Experiment Station in Geneva is another public resource — the largest apple collection in the world, called the National Apple Collection. Maintained by the Agricultural Research Service of the U.S. Department of Agriculture, it is home to thousands of varieties of apples, including varieties of *M. sieversii*, the main progenitor of the commercial apple. Collected from the wild apple forests of central Asia, they have a genetic resistance to diseases that can help apple breeders develop new resistant varieties and rootstocks.

Most of the varieties used for breeding new cultivars of apples in the United States come from what is known as the North America gene pool. Dating back to the seedling orchards planted when settlers first arrived between the seventeenth and nineteenth centuries, this collection is often referred to as the Johnny Appleseed gene pool.

Buying Apples

Apples are available throughout the year in North America. Obviously, weather and latitude play a big part in the distribution of apple orchards across the United States. Varieties that ripen in September in the southern states ripen around November in the north. Because of differences in climate, an apple variety that is sweet and perfumed in Vermont may be flat and mealy in Virginia. In fact, in the north, some apples must be picked before they are mature in order to beat the first frost. Whatever the region, apples that are considered "best keepers" are left to ripen — often becoming sweeter and more flavorful with age — in controlled-atmosphere storage at larger commercial orchards.

Unfortunately, after December, the apples that reach consumers often have been transported long distances and may not have been kept under refrigeration in the grocery

HOW MANY TO BUY

WHEN BUYING JUST ENOUGH APPLES FOR A PIE, 2½ pounds will do it — that's about five large, seven to eight medium, or nine to ten small apples. A medium apple is approximately 3 inches in diameter.

A peck of apples weighs 10½ pounds, and there are 42 pounds in a bushel. It's cheaper to buy a bushel, but if you don't plan to go on an immediate cooking spree (this quantity would make about 16 pies or 20 quarts of applesauce), make sure you can store them until you're ready to use them, or that you have plenty of apple-loving friends.

stores or supermarkets. Some stores may even polish their apples to make them look even more appealing, and this removes the natural bloom. Once this bloom is removed, apples start to break down.

At the orchards, the loads of just-picked apples are so fresh and in such peak condition they haven't had time to bruise. It is for this reason that apple devotees go a little crazy every autumn. Starting as early as August and continuing through November, they make weekend pilgrimages to their local orchards and farm stands, looking for varieties that never reach the village markets or for those orchard jewels of limited production — such as Summer Rambo, Patricia, and Raritan.

Apple Grades

Although most apples are sold loose by the pound, quart, peck, or bushel, some retail stores sell them packaged in perforated plastic bags. The bags are stamped with the weight, variety, and U.S. grade — U.S. Extra Fancy, or U.S. Fancy, with U.S. No. 1 meeting the minimum standards of quality.

Apples are graded mostly according to color and size. A very large, deep-red Red Delicious will be Extra Fancy, while a small, somewhat greenish Red Delicious will be U.S. No. 1. I am frequently disappointed by large, perfect-looking apples. All too often they turn out to be tasteless and mealy.

Orchardists who sell locally grade their apples somewhat differently. Extra Fancy becomes Grade A, and Fancy is called Grade B, seconds, or utility. Grade B apples grow on the inside of the tree and are not as colorful or as large, and sometimes they are not as sweet.

Windfalls or bruised apples are also called utility or Grade 3.

Choosing Apples

There's nothing mystical about choosing apples. As a rule, what you see is what you get. If you bear the following points in mind, you'll end up with some pretty good specimens in your bag:

* Look for apples that are bruise free and firm to the touch. A bruise or blemish on the skin means a decay spot in the flesh.
* Overripe apples will feel soft, and the texture will be mealy or mushy. The background, or undercast, color will be a dull yellow or a dull green instead of a soft light green or yellow.

✳ When the green of an apple is very dark, it is an indication that the apple is not fully mature. Such apples will be hard and sour and have poor flavor. Underripe apples are fine for cooking. If you want them for eating out of hand, refrigerate them and allow them to ripen slowly for a week or two.

Your decision to choose a particular variety should be influenced by what you plan to do with the apples. For the lunch box, you'll want crisp, crunchy, juicy apples. Summer apples that have these qualities include Early Blaze, Ginger Gold, Jonamac, Patricia, Paula Red, and Raritan. Later, I would choose Braeburn, Empire, Fuji, Jonagold, Macoun, McIntosh, and Mutsu/Crispin, among others. If you want to bake apples whole, or make pies, then choose those that hold their shape and retain their flavor, such as Northern Spy, Stayman, Jonathan, Jonagold, Braeburn, and others. (For a complete breakdown of best uses for apples, see page 231.)

To Peel or Not to Peel

There's a lot of goodness in the peel of an apple. It contains vitamin C, fiber, and much of the apple's flavor. So why not leave the skin on for all the recipes? Because some apples have tough skins, and even if the skin is not tough when the apple is eaten raw, it does not break down in the cooking process. Nothing, in my opinion, spoils a fine cake, pudding, or applesauce more than finding some cooked apple skin. You can leave the apple skins on in any of the recipes that call for peeling. Then see how you feel about "to peel or not to peel."

Planning to make gallons of applesauce? Then you may want to invest in a special strainer, available from specialty kitchen stores. For small batches of sauce, a food mill or a food processor does a fine job. I often purée my chunky skin-on applesauce in a food processor and barely notice the flecks of finely processed skin.

If a recipe calls for a lot of chopped or grated vegetables and apples, I use a food processor. When a recipe calls for cubed apples, I always prepare them by hand to make sure I get uniform pieces. A food processor will make very thin and very uniform apple *slices* in no time at all.

Cooking with Apples

As famous as apples are for pie, they can be enjoyed in countless other ways. With just a little imagination, you can use this versatile fruit in almost as many savory recipes as dessert dishes.

Cut into rings, apples can be sautéed along with pork chops and cider. Chopped and sautéed with onions, they elevate such pedestrian

Apple Equivalents					
Size	Diameter in Inches	Sliced or Chopped	Finely Chopped	Grated	Sauce
Large	3¾	2 cups	1½ cups	1¼ cups	¾ cup
Medium	2¾	1⅓ cups	1 cup	¾ cup	½ cup
Small	2¼	¾ cup	¾ cup	½ cup	⅓ cup

fare as braised cabbage and Polish sausage from Sunday's supper to a guest dish. When diced large, they make a delicious addition to any braised chicken recipe or pork and lamb stews. At some time or another, we've all had one of the many variations of apple stuffing with turkey and duck. Apple chutneys, relishes, and sauces can also take their place next to pork, poultry, goose, game, and curries.

For dessert, apples can be stuffed and baked, crisply fritttered, folded into crêpes, mixed into cakes and breads, baked in tarts and pies, and tucked into cobblers and crisps.

Cooking Apples in the Microwave

"BAKED" WHOLE 4 large apples, washed, cored, and scored around the center (this will prevent the apples from bursting). Arrange in a microwave-safe dish (stuff with dried fruit, nuts, honey, and butter as desired). Pour ½ cup apple juice or water into the dish, cover loosely with wax or parchment paper, and microwave on high for 10 minutes. Remove and let sit, covered, for 4 to 5 minutes, until tender.

POACHED SLICES 4 medium apples (about 1 pound), peeled, cored, and sliced ¼ inch thick. Place in a microwave-safe dish. Dissolve ½ cup sugar in 1 cup hot water or apple juice and pour over the apple slices. Cover loosely with wax or parchment paper and microwave on high for 4 minutes, stirring after 2 minutes. Remove and let sit, covered, for 4 to 5 minutes, until tender.

STEWED 4 medium apples (about 1 pound), peeled, cored, and sliced ¼ inch thick. Place in a microwave-safe dish and toss with ½ cup sugar and 1 tablespoon water. Cover loosely with wax or parchment paper and microwave on high for 8 minutes, stirring after 4 minutes. Remove and let sit, covered, for 2 to 4 minutes, until tender.

Preparing Apples with the Food Processor

SLICED Wash or peel apples, cut in half, and remove cores. Place the desired medium or thick slicing disk into the food processor and lock the lid. Snugly stack the apples in the feed chute with cored sides facing the same way. Use the pulse button and gently press down the chute pusher to steadily feed the apples through the slicing disk. Repeat with the rest of the halved apples. After removing the slices, sprinkle with lemon or apple juice (or salad dressing) to prevent browning.

CHOPPED Wash or peel apples, halve, and core. Quarter and cut each into three chunks. Using the metal blade, drop no more than 2 cups of chunks at a time into the processor bowl. Lock on the lid and pulse about three times for a chunky chop and five or six times for a fine chop. Repeat with the rest of the apple chunks. Remove the chopped apples to a bowl and sprinkle with lemon or apple juice to prevent browning.

Storing Apples

Apples ripen 10 times faster in a dry, warm atmosphere than when they are in cold storage. Therefore, commercial orchardists store their apples in controlled-atmosphere sealed chambers. Such storage reduces (without arresting) an apple's intake of oxygen, which slows down its maturation process. This method prolongs the storage life of an apple by several months and enables orchardists to pick apples that are not meant for immediate consumption before they are fully ripe. As they mature slowly in controlled storage, the good keepers retain their juicy, crisp texture while becoming more flavorful and sweeter.

The U.S. Apple Association advises consumers to refrigerate apples in the hydrator drawer at temperatures anywhere from 32 to 40°F.

Some of the best apples for keeping include Cortland, Delicious, Empire, Fuji, Granny Smith, Honeycrisp, Idared, Macoun, McIntosh, Mutsu/Crispin, Northern Spy, Rhode Island Greening, Rome Beauty, Stayman, and Winesap.

Summer apples harvested in July, August, and early September are not good keepers. They must be refrigerated immediately and used within four to six weeks. These include the following varieties: Ginger Gold, Jerseymac, Jonamac, Lodi, Patricia, Paula Red, Puritan, Raritan, Summer Rambo, Tydeman's Red, and Wellington.

When keeping your apples under refrigeration, be sure to store them in perforated plastic bags or containers to prevent them from drying out.

With some varieties, even short exposure to warm temperatures causes overripening, a mealy texture, and loss of flavor. So whether you pick your own apples or buy them in a store, put them into a cool place without delay. However, check first for damaged or bruised apples and set those aside for immediate use. As we all know, a rotten apple in the barrel surely does spoil the whole crop.

Besides refrigeration, other methods of preserving a bounteous harvest include freezing and canning slices and sauce and putting up preserves. See chapter 7 for more information on preserving.

Substituting Apples

I give apple variety recommendations in most of the recipes in this cookbook because some recipes work better with sweet apples, some with tart apples, and some with apples that have a hard texture and don't fall apart. For example, in the Apple Puff Omelet on page 24, I specify two large Cortland, Jonathan, or Idared apples. Any of these would be my first choice because of their flavor and texture. However, if these varieties were not available, I would choose another that had similar qualities. In this case, I would choose Granny Smith apples that were very light green, an indication that they were ripe and only mildly tart (as opposed to dark green and very tart, qualities I would avoid unless I had no other choice and was desperate to make a pie). They also have a good firm texture. Failing that choice, I would then look for Golden Delicious, or Jonagold apples that were more green than yellow, an indication that they were barely ripe and had a firm texture and a more tart flavor than when completely yellow and fully ripe. In fact, my choice would be to combine the light green Granny Smith apples with other firm apples; the combination would provide a more complex flavor. If in doubt, refer to the discussion of apple varieties in chapter 8.

When a recipe calls for one large apple and yours look small to medium, substitute by the cup according to the table on page 17.

CHAPTER 2

Apple Breakfasts & Breads

A good breakfast is touted as the best way to start your day, and what better way to add interest and nutrition to your breakfast than with apples? They go into everything from omelets to pancakes, and they taste great alongside bacon, sausage, and ham. Apples also add both flavor and moistness to a wide variety of breakfast breads, coffee cakes, and baked goods.

BAKED APPLE-CRANBERRY OATMEAL

YIELD: 6–8 servings

This looks soupy when poured into the baking dish. However, the oats really absorb the liquid. I like to pour a little milk on top when it is in my breakfast bowl. In fact, this is a perfect oatmeal to make ahead and refrigerate. Spooned cold into small bowls, sprinkled with flaked coconut and ¼ cup milk, it can be heated in the microwave on high for 30 seconds. Breakfast: ready when you are.

1   Preheat the oven to 350°F. Grease a 7- by 11-inch baking dish.

2   Combine the oats, brown sugar, cranberries, walnuts, apples, cinnamon, and salt in a large bowl.

3   In a medium bowl, beat together the oil and egg, and then whisk in the milk and cider. Stir the liquid mixture into the dry ingredients and spoon the mixture into the prepared baking dish.

4   Bake for 30 to 35 minutes, until set into a firm porridge.

INGREDIENTS

- 2 cups regular or quick-cooking oats
- ½ cup firmly packed brown sugar
- ½ cup dried cranberries, dried cherries, or dried blueberries
- ½ cup chopped walnuts or shredded coconut
- 2 medium apples (Empire, Golden Delicious, McIntosh), peeled, cored, and cut into small dice
- 1½ teaspoons ground cinnamon
- ½ teaspoon sea salt
- 2 tablespoons canola oil or coconut oil
- 1 large egg
- 1½ cups low-fat milk
- ½ cup apple cider or juice

So easy and a little special, this layered treat will be gobbled up for breakfast or as an afternoon snack. Use festive glass sundae dishes or squat 8-ounce drinking glasses and assemble just before serving so that the granola stays crunchy.

granola, APPLESauce & yogurt sundae

YIELD: 4 servings

INGREDIENTS

4 (6-ounce) containers vanilla Greek yogurt

1 cup granola, gluten free if desired

1½ cups Sweet Applesauce (page 176) flavored with 1 teaspoon ground cinnamon

1 Spoon about ¼ cup yogurt into each dish. Add 2 tablespoons granola and top with ¼ cup applesauce.

2 Repeat layering until all ingredients are used.

PASTEURIZING APPLE CIDER

TODAY, MOST FRESH APPLE CIDER OR JUICE IS PASTEURIZED or treated with ultraviolet (UV) light, both processes approved by the Food and Drug Administration. The pasteurization process involves heating the freshly pressed cider or juice to 160°F for a few seconds. At this temperature, any bacteria present are killed. Once 160°F has been reached, the cider is quickly cooled to avoid any change in flavor. The UV treatment involves passing the cider by an ultraviolet light, which kills harmful bacteria. This nonthermal process does not heat the cider and is a safe alternative to pasteurization. Although some people might prefer to drink raw fresh cider or juice, neither of these processes affects flavor or the nutritional values. To avoid the possible presence of pathogens in raw cider, the medical profession recommends that older people and young children, in particular, drink juice that has been pasteurized or UV treated. Juice-producing facilities are inspected regularly by federal and state agencies.

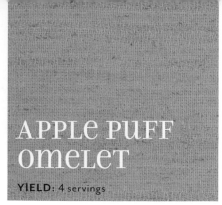

APPLE PUFF OMELET

YIELD: 4 servings

This is a good way to make an omelet for four people so that everyone eats at the same time. You can prepare the apples the night before and heat them in a skillet for a couple of minutes the next morning. You can also keep canned apple slices (page 208) in the pantry and substitute those in a pinch.

1 Preheat the oven to 450°F.

2 Melt the butter in a medium skillet over low heat, and sauté the apples for 5 minutes.

3 Mix the brown sugar and cinnamon. Sprinkle over the apples. Toss and continue to sauté the apples for about 10 minutes, until they caramelize. The mixture will be thick and syrupy. Spoon the mixture into an 8-inch-square baking dish and keep hot in the oven.

4 Whisk the yolks and the granulated sugar in a small bowl until fairly thick.

5 In a large bowl, beat the egg whites with the cream of tartar until stiff and shiny. Fold into the yolk mixture, a third at a time.

6 Pour the egg mixture over the apples and bake for 8 to 10 minutes. The omelet will be puffed and golden. Remove from the oven and sprinkle with the confectioners' sugar. Serve immediately.

INGREDIENTS

- 4 tablespoons butter
- 2 large apples (Cortland, Jonathan, Idared), peeled, cored, and thinly sliced
- ¼ cup firmly packed brown sugar
- 1 teaspoon ground cinnamon
- 4 eggs, separated
- ¼ cup granulated sugar
- ¼ teaspoon cream of tartar
- 1 tablespoon confectioners' sugar

sausage & APPLe omeLeT

YIELD: 2 servings

I have made this omelet with soybean protein "crumbles" and also "veggie ground round." The flavorings and textures are uncannily sausagelike, making these foods good substitutions for the sausage.

INGREDIENTS

2 large fresh sausages, casings removed

3 scallions, white and green parts, sliced

1 medium apple (Granny Smith, Baldwin, Winesap, Empire), peeled, cored, and chopped

1 tablespoon butter

4 eggs

Sea salt and freshly ground black pepper

1 In a medium skillet over medium heat, brown the sausage meat, breaking it up and turning it as it cooks, for about 8 minutes. Drain off most of the fat and push the meat to one side. Add the scallions to the skillet and sauté for 2 minutes.

2 Stir the apple into the sausage mixture and cook over low heat for 5 minutes. Transfer the mixture to a bowl and cover to keep warm.

3 Melt the butter in the same skillet over medium heat. Lightly beat the eggs and season with salt and pepper to taste. Add the eggs to the foaming butter. Shake the pan to spread the eggs. As they set, use a fork to make a zigzag pattern from the edges to the center in several places. Shake the pan to keep the uncooked egg mixture moving.

4 After 2 to 3 minutes, the eggs should be set on the bottom and the top should be creamy. Remove from the heat; spoon the sausage mixture onto one side of the eggs. Fold the other half over the filling and slide the omelet onto a warm plate. Serve immediately.

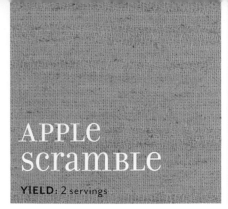

APPLE scramble

YIELD: 2 servings

This is an easy way to have a good breakfast and satisfy a sweet tooth at the same time. It also makes an appetizing after-school snack.

1 In a medium bowl, beat the eggs with the honey. Add the apple. Stir to mix.

2 Heat the butter and oil in a medium skillet over medium heat. When the butter starts to sizzle, pour in the egg mixture.

3 Start stirring immediately with a wooden spoon. Cook for 3 to 4 minutes, or until the eggs are cooked.

4 Serve on buttered toast for breakfast or a hot snack.

INGREDIENTS

2 eggs

1 tablespoon honey

1 medium apple (Granny Smith, Braeburn, Empire), peeled, cored, and grated

1 teaspoon butter

1 teaspoon vegetable oil

Buttered toast for serving

APPLES FOR BREAKFAST AND SNACK ATTACKS

SCHOOL-DAY MORNINGS DEMAND SNACK BREAKFASTS that are nutritious and quick. These "recipes" make fast and easy breakfasts or after-school snacks.

✳ ½ cup yogurt or low-fat cottage cheese topped with ½ cup applesauce (pages 80 and 176) and sprinkled with a favorite cereal.

✳ 1 cup yogurt combined with 2 tablespoons chopped walnuts, 2 tablespoons raisins, and 1 small apple, chopped, topped with 1 tablespoon honey and 1 tablespoon wheat germ.

✳ 1 medium apple, chopped and combined in a bowl with instant oatmeal and milk, as indicated on the packet. Microwave on high as recommended, about 60 seconds. Drizzle with honey, spoon vanilla yogurt over the top, and sprinkle with cinnamon.

✳ 2 slices multigrain or whole-wheat bread spread with peanut butter and topped with thin slices of apple and slices of cheese, toasted in a toaster oven until the cheese begins to melt, about 2 minutes. Sandwich together if eating on the run.

Truly, this is a great way to make a vegetable omelet pie. In fact, a frittata might appear on my table for breakfast, lunch, or even dinner. I may use leftover vegetables or a variety of fresh vegetables in season. It tastes delicious warm or at room temperature and is therefore excellent for a brunch buffet.

APPLE FRITTATA

YIELD: 2–4 servings

INGREDIENTS

- 1 tablespoon olive or canola oil
- 1 medium onion, chopped
- 1 red or green bell pepper, seeds and ribs removed, chopped
- 1 garlic clove, minced
- 1 medium apple (Granny Smith, Empire, Braeburn), peeled, cored, and thinly sliced
- 4 eggs
- 2 tablespoons water
- ½ teaspoon dried sage
- ¼ teaspoon ground mace
- Sea salt and freshly ground black pepper
- ½ cup grated cheddar, Jack, or your favorite melting cheese

1 Heat the oil in a medium skillet over low heat. Add the onion, bell pepper, and garlic, and cook until the onion is tender, about 15 minutes.

2 Add the apple to the vegetables and cook for 5 minutes.

3 Beat the eggs with the water, sage, mace, and salt and pepper to taste. Pour over the vegetables. Sprinkle with the cheese.

4 Cover the pan and cook over low heat for 10 minutes, or until the eggs are set and the cheese has melted. Serve warm or at room temperature.

breakfast sausage crêpes

YIELD: 4 servings

This is one of my husband's favorite breakfasts. I make the crêpes (thin pancakes), and he cooks the sausages. You could also make the crêpes ahead of time and stack them between sheets of wax paper.

1 Sprinkle the apple slices with the cinnamon and mace.

2 Melt the butter in a medium skillet over medium heat; sauté the apples for about 15 minutes, or until soft and golden. Keep warm.

3 Prick the sausages and cook in a greased medium skillet over low heat for about 10 minutes. Keep warm in a low oven or covered on top of the stove.

4 Roll the crêpes around the sausages, top with the sautéed apples, and serve hot with maple syrup.

INGREDIENTS

2 cups Canned Apple Slices (page 208), drained

½ teaspoon ground cinnamon

½ teaspoon ground mace

3 tablespoons butter

8 link sausages, 5–6 inches long

8 crêpes (page 30)

Maple syrup for serving

You may want to use ready-grated mixed cheeses in this recipe. Low-fat cheeses work fine, too; however, avoid the fat-free grated cheeses — they have a rubbery texture when heated.

APPLE-CHEDDAR crêpes

YIELD: 4 servings

INGREDIENTS

- 3 cups Canned Apple Slices (page 208), drained
- ¼ cup apple juice or cider
- ½ teaspoon freshly grated nutmeg or ¼ teaspoon ground
- 8 crêpes (page 30)
- 4 ounces cheddar cheese, grated (1 cup)
- 1 tablespoon butter, melted

1 Combine the apple slices, juice, and nutmeg in a medium skillet and cook over low heat for 10 to 15 minutes, or until the apples are tender and the liquid has almost evaporated.

2 Preheat the oven to 375°F. Lightly grease a shallow 9- by 13-inch baking dish.

3 Fill each crêpe with about ¼ cup of the apple mixture topped with 2 tablespoons or so of the cheese. (Spoon the filling onto the lower third and roll up from the bottom.)

4 Place the crêpes, seam side down, in the prepared dish. Brush with the melted butter and bake for 15 minutes, or until hot.

basic crêpes

YIELD: 8–10 crêpes

This recipe is borrowed from the basic thin pancake recipe made with all milk. For thicker drop pancakes, use 1 cup liquid to 1 cup flour. If you are making dessert crêpes, add 2 tablespoons sugar and 1 teaspoon vanilla extract to the batter ingredients.

1 In a blender or mixing bowl, combine the milk, flour, water, eggs, and oil and beat until smooth.

2 Warm a scant teaspoon of vegetable oil in a medium skillet over medium heat. Pour ¼ cup of the batter into the skillet and tilt until the batter covers the bottom. Cook for 2 minutes, or until the crêpe is golden brown on the bottom. Turn with a spatula and cook for 1 to 2 minutes longer.

3 Repeat with the rest of the batter. Stack the crêpes between sheets of wax paper on a plate and keep warm in a low oven, or serve each one immediately.

INGREDIENTS

1 cup milk

1 cup sifted all-purpose flour

¼ cup water or apple juice

2 eggs

2 tablespoons canola oil or butter, melted

Vegetable oil for frying

When I was growing up in Britain, pancakes were often served for dessert and without fail on Pancake Day or Shrove Tuesday. We squeezed fresh lemon juice over the pancakes and then sprinkled them with sugar.

APPLE pancakes

YIELD: 4–6 servings (16–20 pancakes)

INGREDIENTS

2 cups sifted all-purpose flour

1½ teaspoons baking powder

1 teaspoon baking soda

1 teaspoon ground cinnamon

2 cups sour cream or 1½ cups plain yogurt

¼ cup apple juice or cider

¼ cup sugar or honey

4 tablespoons butter, melted

2 eggs

2 medium apples (McIntosh, Golden Delicious, Empire), peeled, cored, and grated

Vegetable oil for frying

Butter, fresh lemon juice, and sugar for serving (optional)

1 Place the flour, baking powder, baking soda, and cinnamon in a large mixing bowl, blender, or food processor. Add the sour cream, apple juice, sugar, melted butter, and eggs. Beat or blend until smooth. The batter will be very thick. Allow the batter to rest for 30 to 60 minutes.

2 Stir the apples into the batter.

3 Heat a medium skillet over medium-high heat and grease with approximately 1 teaspoon of vegetable oil. Drop the batter onto the hot skillet a few tablespoons at a time (for larger pancakes, measure ¼ cup batter).

4 When bubbles appear on top after approximately 2 minutes, turn and brown the other side, about 2 minutes. Serve with butter, lemon juice, and sugar, if desired.

PANCAKE GÂTEAU

LAYER CANNED OR COOKED APPLE SLICES WITH A STACK OF PANCAKES to make a "gâteau," and drizzle the layers with melted preserves. To do this, make at least six thin 8- or 9-inch pancakes, cover one side with fruit spread, such as raspberry, apricot, or marmalade, and make layers with the apple slices in a baking dish. Bake at 350°F for 20 minutes, or until hot. Serve drizzled with melted preserves and with a scoop of frozen vanilla yogurt or ice cream.

APPLe-corn HOTcakes

Great for breakfast, these tasty, savory hotcakes can also replace bread or a side dish at dinner. The hotcakes are quite filling; often one or two per person will suffice. Leftover hotcakes can be crumbled and used as stuffing for Cornish game hens or chicken.

1 Melt the butter in a medium skillet over medium heat, and sauté the apple and scallion for 3 minutes.

2 In a large bowl, mix the cornmeal, flour, baking powder, baking soda, mace, cayenne, and salt and pepper to taste. Make a well in the center.

3 In a small bowl, beat the milk, cheese, and egg. Add the sautéed apple and scallion. Pour into the well of the dry ingredients and stir to combine.

4 Heat approximately 1 teaspoon vegetable oil on a griddle or in a large skillet over medium heat. When the oil is hot, drop ¼ cup of the batter onto the griddle and cook for 2 minutes, or until the hotcakes are golden on the bottom. Turn and cook for 3 minutes longer. Serve immediately with butter, or keep warm in the oven.

INGREDIENTS

1 tablespoon butter or canola oil

1 medium apple (Granny Smith, Idared, Golden Delicious), peeled, cored, and finely chopped

1 scallion, white and pale green parts, thinly sliced

¾ cup yellow cornmeal

¼ cup sifted all-purpose flour

½ teaspoon baking powder

½ teaspoon baking soda

½ teaspoon ground mace

⅛ teaspoon ground cayenne pepper

Sea salt and freshly ground black pepper

¾ cup milk

2 ounces cheddar cheese, grated (½ cup)

1 egg

Vegetable oil for frying

Butter for serving

Fritters are a treat for any time of day, and they are a snap to make. To keep them crunchy, not soggy, cook them on high heat and don't crowd the skillet. Drizzle hot fritters with warm syrup or dust them with confectioners' sugar.

GRATED-APPLE FRITTERS

YIELD: 2–4 servings (12–16 fritters)

INGREDIENTS

- 1 large apple (Rome Beauty, Fuji, Jonagold, Mutsu/Crispin), peeled, cored, and grated
- 2 eggs
- ½ cup sifted all-purpose flour
- ½ teaspoon baking powder
- ½ teaspoon baking soda
- ½ teaspoon ground cinnamon
- ½ teaspoon freshly grated or ground nutmeg
- Vegetable oil for deep-frying

1 Place the apple in a medium bowl.

2 Separate the eggs. Drop the whites into a large bowl, the yolks into a small one. Whisk the yolks until light and stir into the grated apple. Add the flour, baking powder, baking soda, cinnamon, and nutmeg, and stir to combine.

3 Beat the egg whites until stiff and fold into the apple mixture.

4 Heat ¼ inch of vegetable oil in a medium skillet over medium-high heat. Drop the batter by heaping tablespoons into the hot oil. Cook for about 1 minute, turn, and cook the other side for the same length of time, until the fritters are golden brown. Drain on absorbent paper and serve immediately, or keep warm in a low oven.

APPLE-RING FRITTERS

YIELD: 4–6 servings (24–30 fritters)

These apple-ring fritters taste good at any time of day. You don't have to let the batter rest for too long, but even a short resting time seems to make the fritters puffier.

1 Combine 1¼ cups of the flour with the beer, sugar, canola oil, and egg yolks in a blender or food processor. Blend until smooth. Transfer to a large bowl. Cover and leave at room temperature for at least 1 hour.

2 Pour at least 2 inches of vegetable oil into a large wok or skillet. Heat to 375°F.

3 In a large bowl, beat the egg whites until stiff. Stir the batter and fold in the egg whites.

4 With the remaining ¼ cup flour, coat both sides of the apple rings, then dip them in the batter. Fry a few at a time for 2 to 3 minutes on each side, until golden brown. Drain on absorbent paper.

5 For the sauce, mix the applesauce, maple syrup, and cinnamon together in a small bowl.

6 Sprinkle the fritters with confectioners' sugar and serve the Apple Maple Sauce on the side.

INGREDIENTS

- 1½ cups sifted all-purpose flour
- 1 cup beer
- 1 tablespoon sugar
- 1 tablespoon canola oil
- 2 eggs, separated
- 2 cups vegetable oil
- 5 large apples (Rome Beauty, Mutsu/Crispin), peeled, cored, and cut into ½-inch rings
- Confectioners' sugar

APPLE MAPLE SAUCE

- 2 cups applesauce
- ⅓ cup maple syrup
- 1 teaspoon ground cinnamon

NEXT BIG THING, A GROWERS' COOPERATIVE

NEXT BIG THING IS A 45-MEMBER cooperative of growers from five states — Washington, Minnesota, Wisconsin, Michigan and New York — and two Canadian provinces — Quebec and Nova Scotia. Next Big Thing is committed to bringing great, high-quality managed fruit varieties, including SweeTango, to market using sustainable farming practices that help reduce food miles. The cooperative arrangement helps ensure that rigorous quality standards are followed in order to provide consumers with the best possible eating experience.

APPLE DOUGHNUTS

If you have kids who like to help out in the kitchen, this is a good recipe to get them interested in bread making. Nothing beats eating bready little doughnuts you have made yourself.

1   In a large bowl, combine the flour, baking powder, baking soda, and cinnamon. Make a well in the center.

2   In a small bowl, cream the sugar and butter until fluffy. Beat in the egg. Add the apple juice, milk, and vanilla, and beat until combined. Pour into the well of the dry ingredients and stir until smooth. Stir the apple into the batter. Cover and chill the dough for 1 hour.

3   Place the dough on a floured board, knead lightly, and roll out to approximately ⅜ inch thick. Cut with a floured 2½-inch doughnut cutter. Reroll scraps and cut a few more.

4   Pour at least 2 inches of oil into a large wok or skillet and heat to 375°F. Without crowding, fry the doughnuts for 1 to 2 minutes on each side, until golden brown. Repeat until all the doughnuts have been fried, reheating the oil to temperature as necessary. Drain on paper towels.

Variation
Sift 1 cup confectioners' sugar with 1 tablespoon ground cinnamon, and sprinkle over the warm doughnuts.

INGREDIENTS

2½ cups sifted all-purpose flour

1½ teaspoons baking powder

1 teaspoon baking soda

½ teaspoon ground cinnamon

½ cup sugar

3 tablespoons butter, softened

1 egg

¼ cup apple juice or cider

¼ cup milk

1 tablespoon vanilla extract

1 medium apple (McIntosh, Golden Delicious, Empire), peeled, cored, and finely chopped

2 cups vegetable oil

APPLE-banana Bread

YIELD: 10–12 servings

Like bananas, apples add moisture to cakes and breads. The flavor here is classic banana, but you can spice it up by adding ½ teaspoon each of ground cinnamon and ground ginger.

1 Preheat the oven to 350°F. Grease and flour an 8- by 4-inch loaf pan.

2 In a large mixing bowl, combine the flour, baking powder, and baking soda. Make a well in the center.

3 Place the bananas in a medium bowl. Beat in the brown sugar, oil, and eggs. Pour into the well of the dry ingredients and stir until just combined.

4 Fold the apple into the batter. Pour into the prepared pan.

5 Bake for about 1 hour, or until a skewer inserted into the center of the loaf comes out clean. Cool in the pan for 10 minutes, then finish cooling on a wire rack.

INGREDIENTS

- 1¾ cups sifted all-purpose flour
- 2 teaspoons baking powder
- ½ teaspoon baking soda
- 2–3 ripe bananas, mashed (1 cup)
- ½ cup firmly packed brown sugar
- ⅓ cup canola oil
- 2 eggs
- 1 medium apple (Honeycrisp, Gala, Golden Delicious, Braeburn), peeled, cored, and diced

Apple Breakfasts & Breads

LOUISE SALINGER'S APPLE TEA BREAD

YIELD: 12 servings

This is a lovely quick bread worthy of any afternoon tea, and because it freezes well, you can always have some on hand.

INGREDIENTS

- ¾ cup sugar
- 4 tablespoons butter, softened
- 2 eggs
- 2 cups all-purpose flour
- 1 teaspoon baking powder
- 1 teaspoon baking soda
- 2 large apples (Winesap, Fuji, Honeycrisp, Braeburn), peeled, cored, and grated (about 2½ cups)
- ¾ cup chopped walnuts
- 1 tablespoon fresh lemon juice
- 1 teaspoon grated lemon zest
- Butter or cream cheese for serving

1   Preheat the oven to 350°F. Grease and flour an 8- by 4-inch loaf pan.

2   In a large bowl, cream the sugar and butter until fluffy. Beat in the eggs. Sift in the flour, baking powder, and baking soda. Stir to combine. Add the apples, walnuts, lemon juice, and lemon zest. Mix thoroughly. Pour into the prepared pan.

3   Bake for 1 hour, or until a skewer inserted into the center of the loaf comes out clean. Cool in the pan for 10 minutes, then finish cooling on a wire rack.

4   Serve at room temperature with a little butter or cream cheese on the slices.

WHOLE-WHEAT & NUT QUICK BREAD

YIELD: 12–14 servings

This bread is packed with such nutritional goodness, eating a slice makes you feel as though you're doing your body a real favor. Eat it for breakfast, as a snack, or at lunch. For a dinner bread, substitute a mix of herbs such as basil, thyme, and oregano for the allspice and cloves.

1   Preheat the oven to 350°F. Grease and flour a 9- by 5-inch loaf pan.

2   In a large bowl, combine the flour, bran, wheat germ, allspice, baking powder, baking soda, and cloves. Make a well in the center.

3   In a small bowl, mix together the apple juice, apple-sauce, yogurt, honey, oil, and eggs. Beat well and pour into the well of the dry ingredients. Stir to combine without overmixing.

4   Fold in the nuts and spoon the batter into the prepared pan. Bake for 50 to 55 minutes, or until a skewer inserted into the center of the loaf comes out clean. Cool in the pan for 10 minutes, then finish cooling on a wire rack.

INGREDIENTS

- 2 cups whole-wheat flour
- ¼ cup bran flakes
- ¼ cup wheat germ
- 2 teaspoons ground allspice
- 2 teaspoons baking powder
- 1 teaspoon baking soda
- ¼ teaspoon ground cloves
- ½ cup apple juice or cider
- ½ cup Unsweetened Applesauce (page 80)
- ½ cup plain or vanilla yogurt
- ⅓ cup honey
- ⅓ cup canola oil
- 2 eggs
- 1 cup chopped walnuts

I met Barbara many years ago when she was working at Haight Orchards in Croton Falls, New York. We used to trade recipes, and this is one of hers that I cherish. She would make up the breads as holiday gifts — such a nice idea that I have often done the same. The bread's round shape adds to its appeal.

BARBARA MULLIN'S COFFEE CAN BREAD

YIELD: 3 cakes (about 8 servings each)

INGREDIENTS

- 4 medium apples (Cortland, Northern Spy, Winesap, Braeburn), peeled, cored, and cut into small dice
- 2 cups sugar
- 1 cup coarsely chopped pecans
- 3 cups all-purpose flour
- 2 teaspoons baking soda
- 1 teaspoon ground cinnamon
- ½ teaspoon ground allspice
- ½ teaspoon freshly grated or ground nutmeg
- 1 cup (2 sticks) butter
- 1 tablespoon vanilla extract
- 2 eggs

1 Preheat the oven to 325°F. Grease and flour three 1-pound coffee cans. Tie a double band of aluminum foil around the cans to extend 2 inches above their tops. Grease the insides of the foil.

2 Place the apples in a large bowl. Add the sugar and pecans and stir to combine.

3 Sift in the flour, baking soda, cinnamon, allspice, and nutmeg. Mix well.

4 Melt the butter in a small saucepan over low heat and stir in the vanilla. Remove from the heat.

5 Lightly beat the eggs. Stir the eggs and butter into the apple mixture.

6 Spoon the batter into the cans. Bake for 1 hour and 15 minutes, or until a skewer inserted into the center of the bread comes out clean. Cool in the cans for 10 minutes, then finish cooling on a wire rack.

APPLE COFFEE CAKE

YIELD: 15–20 servings

This is a lovely company's-coming cake. You might want to drizzle it with the Apple Glaze on page 169.

1 Preheat the oven to 350°F. Grease and flour a 10-inch tube pan.

2 Place the apples in a large bowl and toss with the lemon juice and the 1 teaspoon cinnamon.

3 In a large bowl, cream the granulated sugar and butter until fluffy. Beat in the eggs, sour cream, and vanilla.

4 In a medium bowl, sift together the flour, baking powder, and baking soda. Fold into the sour cream mixture. Stir in the apples. Pour half of this batter into the prepared pan.

5 In a small bowl, mix the 1 tablespoon cinnamon with the brown sugar and pecans. Sprinkle over the batter in the pan. Cover with the rest of the batter and smooth the top.

6 Bake for 1 hour and 20 minutes, or until a skewer inserted into the cake comes out clean. Cool in the pan for 10 minutes, then finish cooling on a wire rack.

INGREDIENTS

- 3 medium apples (Golden Delicious, Gala, Braeburn, Empire), peeled, cored, and finely chopped
- Juice of ½ lemon
- 1 teaspoon plus 1 tablespoon ground cinnamon
- 2 cups granulated sugar
- 1 cup (2 sticks) butter, softened
- 4 eggs
- 1 cup sour cream
- 1 tablespoon vanilla extract
- 2½ cups all-purpose flour
- 1 teaspoon baking powder
- 1 teaspoon baking soda
- ½ cup firmly packed brown sugar
- 1 cup chopped pecans

Bran-APPLESAUCE MUFFINS

YIELD: 12–18 muffins

These are my weight-watching muffins. They have such a good flavor, satisfy my sweet tooth, and make me feel terribly virtuous. That is, if I eat only one! And because they come together so fast, I can mix and bake them first thing in the morning and have one (or two) for breakfast.

1 Preheat the oven to 400°F. Grease 12 large or 18 small muffin cups.

2 In a large bowl, stir together the all-purpose flour, whole-wheat flour, bran, baking powder, baking soda, cinnamon, nutmeg, and cloves.

3 Make a well in the center of the dry ingredients and add the applesauce and oil.

4 In a small bowl, beat together the honey and eggs and add to the well in the center of the bran mixture. Stir together just until the dry ingredients are moist (a lumpy mixture makes tender muffins).

5 Fill each muffin cup approximately two-thirds full. Bake for 18 to 20 minutes, or until a skewer inserted into the center of a muffin comes out clean. Remove from the muffin cups immediately and cool on a wire rack, or serve warm.

INGREDIENTS

1 cup all-purpose flour

½ cup whole-wheat flour

1 cup bran flakes

2 teaspoons baking powder

1 teaspoon baking soda

1 teaspoon ground cinnamon

½ teaspoon freshly grated or ground nutmeg

¼ teaspoon ground cloves

1 cup Sweet Applesauce (page 176)

⅓ cup canola oil

½ cup honey

2 eggs

APPLESAUCE MUFFINS

YIELD: 12 muffins

This is a great way to use up applesauce and juice — and an easy way to include more fruit in your diet!

INGREDIENTS

- 1 cup all-purpose flour
- 1 cup white whole-wheat flour
- 2 teaspoons baking powder
- ½ teaspoon baking soda
- 1 teaspoon ground cinnamon
- ¼–½ teaspoon five-spice powder
- 2 eggs
- 1 cup honey, or ½ cup molasses and ½ cup honey
- ¼ cup canola oil
- ½ cup apple cider or juice
- 1 cup chunky Unsweetened Applesauce (page 80); if using smooth sauce, cut back to ¾ cup

1 Preheat the oven to 375°F. Grease a 12-cup muffin pan.

2 In a large bowl, stir together the all-purpose flour, whole-wheat flour, baking powder, baking soda, cinnamon, and five-spice powder to taste. Make a well in the center.

3 In a medium bowl, beat together the eggs, honey, oil, and cider. Stir in the applesauce. Pour into the well of the dry ingredients and stir together just until combined.

4 Divide the batter among the muffin cups. The cups will be almost full. Bake on the middle rack for 18 to 20 minutes, or until a skewer inserted into the center of a muffin comes out clean. Cool in the pan for 5 minutes, then finish cooling on a wire rack.

APPLE MUFFINS with carrot & coconut

YIELD: 12 muffins

I frequently eat muffins for breakfast, and those containing coconut are my favorite — to the point where I often throw ½ to 1 cup shredded coconut into any muffin recipe I make. If I have leftover coconut milk (I use it to cook chicken, seafood, and rice), that also goes into my muffins. I prefer low-fat coconut milk because in the full-fat version the cream settles on the top and needs to be blended into the separated liquid. Almond milk would be a good alternative in this recipe, but low-fat dairy milk is fine, too.

1 Preheat the oven to 375°F. Grease a 12-cup muffin pan.

2 In a large bowl, stir together the all-purpose flour, whole-wheat flour, baking powder, cinnamon, and ginger. Make a well in the center.

3 In a medium bowl, beat together the honey, coconut milk, oil, and eggs. Stir in the apple, carrot, and coconut. Pour into the well of the dry ingredients and stir together just until combined.

4 Divide the batter among the muffin cups. The cups will be almost full. Bake on the middle rack for 18 to 20 minutes, or until a skewer inserted into the center of a muffin comes out clean. Cool in the pan for 5 minutes, then finish cooling on a wire rack.

INGREDIENTS

- 1½ cups all-purpose flour
- ½ cup white whole-wheat flour
- 2 teaspoons baking powder
- 1½ teaspoons ground cinnamon
- ½ teaspoon ground ginger
- 1 cup honey
- ¾ cup low-fat coconut milk
- ¼ cup canola or coconut oil
- 2 eggs
- 1 medium apple (Gala, Golden Delicious, Braeburn), peeled, cored, and grated (½–¾ cup)
- 1 carrot, scrubbed and grated (½–¾ cup)
- ½ cup shredded coconut, sweetened or unsweetened as preferred

APPLESAUCE & WHOLE-WHEAT YEAST ROLLS

YIELD: 12 rolls

These sweet rolls are not 100 percent whole wheat, but they're hearty and tasty with the addition of bran flakes and walnuts.

1 Grease a 12-cup muffin pan.

2 In a large bowl, stir together the all-purpose flour, whole-wheat flour, bran, walnuts, yeast, and salt. Make a well in the center.

3 Melt the butter in a small saucepan over low heat. Add the honey and milk and heat until an instant-read or candy thermometer registers between 120 and 130°F and the honey has dissolved. Remove from the heat. Stir in the applesauce. Pour into the well of the dry ingredients and stir until combined.

4 Spoon ¼ to ⅓ cup batter into each muffin cup. Place in a warm, draft-free place and cover loosely with plastic wrap. Let rise until doubled in size, about 40 minutes.

5 Preheat the oven to 350°F.

6 Bake on the middle rack for 20 to 25 minutes, or until golden or a thermometer inserted into the center of a roll reads 195 to 200°F.

7 Remove the rolls from the muffin cups and serve warm, or cool completely and place in a resealable plastic bag. They will stay fresh in the bag for 2 days, or freeze for up to 3 months.

INGREDIENTS

- 1 cup all-purpose flour
- 1 cup white or brown whole-wheat flour
- 1 cup bran flakes
- ½ cup chopped walnuts
- 2 packets rapid-rise yeast
- 1 teaspoon sea salt
- ½ cup (1 stick) butter
- ¾ cup honey
- ½ cup low-fat milk
- 1 cup Unsweetened Applesauce (page 80)

While a fresh muffin or a slice of quick bread can be perfectly delicious without a swipe of butter or jam, I have to admit to having a weakness for cream cheese — and even more so when it is combined with a little honey, preserves, or other naturally sweet ingredient. It's the perfect frosting on my breakfast breads. Using a low-fat (Neufchâtel) cream cheese doesn't compromise the flavor or texture, but it certainly does keep the saturated fat content quite a bit lower.

THREE BREAKFAST SPREADS

HONEY CREAM CHEESE SPREAD

YIELD: 1¾ cups

> 8 ounces low-fat cream cheese, softened
>
> ¼ cup honey
>
> 1 teaspoon grated orange or lemon zest

In a small bowl, combine the cream cheese, honey, and orange zest. Beat well.

APRICOT CREAM CHEESE SPREAD

YIELD: 1 cup

> 8 ounces low-fat cream cheese, softened
>
> ¼ cup apricot preserves, or any thick jam

In a small bowl, combine the cream cheese and preserves. Beat well.

APPLE-DATE CREAM CHEESE SPREAD

YIELD: 1¼ cups

> 1 cup finely chopped pitted dates
>
> ½ cup apple juice or cider
>
> 8 ounces low-fat cream cheese, softened

1   In a small saucepan, cook the dates in the apple juice over low heat, stirring, until the mixture thickens, about 5 minutes. Set aside to cool.

2   In a small bowl, beat the cream cheese until fluffy. Beat the cooled date mixture into the cream cheese. Chill and serve.

CHAPTER 3

Apple Drinks & Snacks

"An apple a day keeps the doctor away." So the old saying goes. If that's the case, you can feel healthy and food smart whenever you snack on an apple or pour yourself a drink of cider or apple juice. If you are looking for something a little more elaborate, think of apple tea, punch, or wassail for a special drink. Substitute apple slices for crackers, bread, or chips. No matter how you serve them, apples are tasty and refreshing.

Iced Apple Tea

YIELD: 6 cups

I love green teas, particularly those flavored with honey, lemon, or mint. I choose basic, unflavored green tea, however, when making iced tea because I enjoy using my own flavorings. Adding apple juice turns it into a drink that is reminiscent of the apple teas, both hot and cold, served in Turkey.

1 Place the tea bags in a pitcher and cover with the boiling water. Allow to steep for 5 minutes.

2 Squeeze the tea bags gently and discard. Stir in the honey, if desired, until dissolved. Stir in the apple juice. Chill (or add a couple of ice cubes to each glass).

3 Pour into four tall glasses and drop a slice of lemon and a sprig of mint into each.

INGREDIENTS

- 4 tea bags (green, orange pekoe, or herbal)
- 4 cups boiling water
- 1 tablespoon honey (optional)
- 2 cups chilled apple juice or cider
- 4 lemon slices
- 4 fresh mint sprigs

FREEZING CIDER

CIDER FREEZES WELL. If you have space in your freezer, you might consider buying extra of your favorite fresh sweet cider in the fall to carry you through until the orchards reopen.

With so many thick, puréed fruit and vegetable drinks available today, it's not so difficult to achieve the recommended daily servings of these foods. Try your hand at making your own drinks; it's far less expensive than buying smoothies and green drinks. Whatever you mix up in your kitchen will not have the same shelf life as a commercial product, so drink it up in two to three days.

TRIPLE APPLE, FRUIT & VEG SHAKE

YIELD: about 6 cups

INGREDIENTS

- 2 medium sweet apples (Gala, Golden Delicious), peeled, cored, and cut into chunks
- 1–2 bananas, sliced (yellow ripe, not brown)
- 2 ripe kiwis, peeled and sliced
- 1 cup pineapple or cantaloupe chunks
- 1 cup young, tender spinach leaves or heart of celery with leaves
- 1 ripe avocado, peeled and pitted
- 1 cup Unsweetened Applesauce (page 80)
- 1 cup apple juice
- ½ cup orange juice
- ¼–½ cup honey

Place the apples, bananas, kiwis, pineapple, spinach, avocado, applesauce, apple juice, orange juice, and honey to taste in a large blender and purée until completely smooth. Taste and adjust to your palate with additional banana and/or honey. To thin, add more apple juice or orange juice, or 6 to 10 ice cubes.

FRESH APPLE & MANGO SMOOTHIE

YIELD: about 5 cups

When I was running kids' camps at my farm, my assistant, Melanie, would freeze bananas and strawberries before she left for home. The next day she would blend fruit and yogurt smoothies and hand them out for a midmorning snack break. This one was always a favorite.

Place the apple, banana, mango, strawberries, honey to taste, milk, yogurt, and ice cubes in a blender and purée until smooth.

INGREDIENTS

1 large sweet apple, peeled, cored, and cut into chunks

1 banana, sliced (yellow ripe, not brown)

1 mango, peeled, pitted, and cut into chunks

10 strawberries, hulled

⅓–½ cup honey

½ cup low-fat milk

1 cup low-fat vanilla yogurt

1 cup ice cubes

APPLE COCKTAILS

Pineapples have long been a symbol of hospitality, and they team well with apples for a refreshing punch. If pineapple is not available, orange segments and juice would be a nice substitute. Orange juice would also be a good swap for the lemon juice in the Apple Cider Sidecar from Patty Power at Distillery Lane Ciderworks.

PARTY APPLE PUNCH

YIELD: about 6 cups

1 small pineapple or 2 (8-ounce) cans unsweetened pineapple chunks or rings

2 medium apples (Red Delicious), peeled, cored, and cut into ¼-inch slices

3 cups sparkling cider or sparkling white wine

2 cups apple juice

1 cup pineapple juice

½ cup brandy, applejack, or vodka

1 Peel and core the pineapple. Coarsely chop the fruit and place it in a large saucepan. If you are using canned pineapple, drain the juice, reserving 1 cup for step 2.

2 Add the apples to the pan along with the sparkling cider, apple juice, and pineapple juice. Heat over low heat for 5 to 10 minutes, or until steaming. Remove the pan from the heat and stir in the liquor. Let the mixture cool slightly and pour into a punch bowl or pitcher. Serve warm or cold, with or without the fruit.

THE APPLE CIDER SIDECAR

YIELD: 4 servings

10 ounces fresh cider (refrigerated, not from concentrate)

5 ounces Cointreau or Triple Sec

3 ounces brandy

2 ounces fresh lemon juice

Sugar for coating

1 lemon, cut in half

1 Fill a cocktail shaker with ice and pour in the cider, Cointreau, brandy, and lemon juice. Shake well.

2 Pour some sugar onto a small plate. Moisten the rims of 4 martini glasses with the lemon halves. Dip the rims into the sugar, and strain the cocktails into the sugar-rimmed martini glasses.

To avoid the possible problem of salmonella, it's wise to avoid using raw eggs. The easiest way to do this is to use a pasteurized egg product if you can't find commercial whole pasteurized eggs.

APPLE EGGNOG

YIELD: 7 cups (about 18 servings)

INGREDIENTS

- ½ cup pasteurized egg product (equivalent to 4 whole eggs), or 4 pasteurized whole eggs
- ½ cup sugar
- 1 cup brandy
- ⅓ cup rum
- 2 cups apple juice or cider
- 3 cups heavy cream
- ½ teaspoon freshly grated nutmeg

1 Place the egg product in a large punch bowl and beat until frothy. Add the sugar and beat until well incorporated and frothy. Beat in the brandy and rum, a little at a time, then the apple juice. Continue beating and add 1 cup of the cream. Beat for several minutes, or until the mixture thickens somewhat.

2 In a medium bowl, beat the remaining 2 cups heavy cream until almost stiff. Stir into the brandy and cream mixture.

3 Sprinkle the nutmeg over the top. Serve at once.

wassail

YIELD: 4 servings

An old Twelfth Night tradition, this medieval drink of wassail (from the Old Norse ves heill, meaning "Be well," a salutation offered when presenting a cup of wine to a guest), or "lamb's wool," as it is also known, is still served in some English homes around Christmas. It is sometimes served with a spoon for eating the baked apple that flavors the beverage.

1 Preheat the oven to 350°F.

2 Slit the skins of the apples horizontally about halfway down. Place in a greased baking dish and sprinkle with the ¼ cup brown sugar and the apple juice. Bake, basting frequently, for about 40 minutes, or until the apples are soft. Remove from the oven. Set out four large mugs and spoon one apple into each.

3 Pour the ale and sherry into a large saucepan. Stir in the 2 tablespoons brown sugar, the cinnamon, ginger, nutmeg, and lemon zest. Cook over low heat for 5 minutes.

4 Pour the warm liquids over the apples. When the wassail has been consumed, take a spoon and eat the apple, if desired.

INGREDIENTS

- 4 medium apples (McIntosh)
- ¼ cup plus 2 tablespoons firmly packed brown sugar
- ¼ cup apple juice or cider
- 3 (12-ounce) bottles ale
- 1 cup sherry
- 1 cinnamon stick
- ½ teaspoon ground ginger
- ½ teaspoon freshly grated nutmeg
- Zest of 1 lemon

This is my mother's adaptation of an Indonesian recipe that calls for chicken livers. She preferred the texture and flavor of sausage. I like to use spicy Cajun or andouille sausage or sometimes a milder chicken and apple sausage. They are all good with the crunchy apple slices.

APPLE & SAUSAGE BUNDLES

YIELD: approximately 24 bundles (6 servings)

INGREDIENTS

MARINADE

- ½ cup apple juice or cider
- 2 tablespoons creamy peanut butter
- 2 tablespoons soy sauce
- ½ teaspoon ground cinnamon
- ½ teaspoon ground ginger

SAUSAGE BUNDLES

- 4 precooked sausages, each about 6 inches long
- 2 medium apples (McIntosh, Golden Delicious)
- 8 ounces bacon

1 For the marinade, put the apple juice, peanut butter, soy sauce, cinnamon, and ginger in a blender or food processor and blend until smooth. Pour into a medium bowl.

2 For the sausage bundles, cut the sausages into 1-inch pieces. Add to the marinade, cover, and refrigerate for 30 minutes or longer.

3 Peel and core the apples and cut them into the same number of slices as there are sausage pieces. (The slices should not be thinner than ¼ inch.)

4 Remove the sausage pieces and drain, reserving the marinade.

5 Cut the bacon strips in half crosswise. Make bundles by wrapping a strip of bacon around a slice of apple and a piece of sausage. Secure with wooden toothpicks. Drop each bundle into the bowl to coat with the marinade.

6 Place the bacon bundles on a broiler rack and broil 4 inches from the heat. Broil approximately 3 minutes per side, watching them carefully and turning them until the bacon is uniformly cooked and crispy.

onion & APPLE samosas

YIELD: 24 samosas

Make these savory turnovers with basic short-crust pastry or thawed purchased puff pastry — they're delicious either way.

1 Preheat the oven to 425°F. Lightly grease two baking sheets or line them with parchment paper.

2 Heat the oil in a large skillet over medium-high heat. Add the onions and garam masala and stir to combine. Sauté for 5 minutes. Stir in the apples and sauté for 5 minutes, then stir in the brown sugar. Reduce the heat to medium and cook until the mixture is golden and somewhat caramelized, about 15 minutes.

3 Stir in the vinegar and cook 5 minutes longer. Remove from the heat and allow the mixture to cool.

4 Remove the puff pastry from the refrigerator and roll out two of the 9- by 9½-inch sheets to 12 by 12 inches. Prick the sheets all over with a fork. Cut 12 squares from each sheet (the squares will be about 3 by 4 inches) and place 12 on each baking sheet.

5 Place 2 to 3 tablespoons of the filling in the center of the 12 squares. Take care not to overfill the squares. Sprinkle about 2 teaspoons cheese over the filling.

6 Cover the filled squares with the remaining squares and, using the tines of a fork, firmly seal the edges. Cut a slit in the top of each samosa.

7 Repeat the rolling and filling process with the remaining two pastry sheets.

8 Refrigerate or freeze for 15 minutes so that the dough is cool and firm before going into the hot oven. Bake on upper and middle racks for 20 to 25 minutes, or until golden and puffed. After 15 minutes, rotate the baking sheets from upper to middle rack and from back to front.

INGREDIENTS

- 1 tablespoon olive, grapeseed, or canola oil
- 2 medium sweet or red onions, cut into quarters and thinly sliced
- 1 teaspoon garam masala, or ½ teaspoon each ground cinnamon and ground cumin with a few grindings of black pepper
- 2 medium apples (Gala, Golden Delicious, Jonagold), peeled, cored, cut into quarters, and thinly sliced crosswise
- 2 tablespoons brown sugar
- 2 tablespoons cider or malt vinegar
- 2 packets (4 sheets) frozen puff pastry, thawed in the refrigerator and kept cold
- 8 ounces shredded cheddar cheese or crumbled goat or feta cheese (2 cups)

APPLE snacks

Forget the bread, crackers, and cookies — substitute apple rings instead. Topped with a variety of spreads, cheeses, and meats, they provide a welcome change on the hors d'oeuvre platter. They are particularly successful with children and health-conscious adults. Topping ideas are described below.

Wash and core apples and cut into ¼-inch to ½-inch slices. Use Ginger Gold or Cameo apples, which are naturally slow to brown. Sprinkle the slices with lemon juice or drop them into a bowl of cold water with 2 tablespoons of lemon juice. Remove and pat dry with paper towels.

Depending on whether you are making snacks, lunch, or hors d'oeuvres, choose from among the following toppings:

Peanut butter with: banana slices or raisins or applesauce or crumbled bacon or chopped nuts

Cream cheese and chutney

Cream cheese with onion slices and smoked salmon (or sardines)

Cream cheese, cinnamon, and honey

Cream cheese with diced ham, curry powder, and chutney

Mashed blue cheese

Hummus

Olive tapenade

Roasted red pepper tapenade

HAVE AN APPLE, CHEESE, AND WINE PARTY

MANY A TIME, THE URGE TO THROW A PARTY has been quashed by the thought of all the preparation involved. One of the easiest ways to resolve this is to choose an apple, cheese, and wine theme. Accompany the apples, cheeses, and wines with an assortment of crusty breads, water biscuits, and crackers.

Buy a good selection of fresh, firm apples, and then choose the cheeses and wines. Identify each apple variety and stack them in baskets next to complementary cheeses and wines. Here are some suggestions:

✳ Golden Delicious or York apples with Edam, mild cheddar, Camembert, or Brie. Drink Médoc or Beaujolais red wines.

✳ Jonathan or Braeburn apples with Scottish Dunlop (cheddar), Gruyère, or provolone. Drink Bardolino or Valpolicella red wines, or Orvieto or Vouvray white wines.

✳ Empire or Gala apples with Muenster, Fontina, or Bel Paese. Drink Soave white or rosé wines.

✳ Macoun or Honeycrisp apples with Caprice des Dieux, Excelsior, or Boursault. Drink Moselle, Graves, or Pouilly white wines, or Côte de Beaune red wines.

APPLE-CHEESE SPREAD

In this recipe I use low-fat cream cheese because I find there is little to distinguish its flavor or texture from that of the whole-fat version, but I do use freshly grated, full-fat cheddar, because I prefer the rich nutty flavor. If you have fresh herbs, substitute 1 tablespoon of chopped herbs for each teaspoon of dried.

YIELD: 2½ cups

INGREDIENTS

- 8 ounces low-fat cream cheese, softened
- 4 ounces cheddar cheese, grated (1 cup)
- 2 tablespoons brandy or sherry
- 1 medium tart apple (Granny Smith), peeled, cored, and grated (½–¾ cup)
- 1 teaspoon dried basil
- 1 teaspoon dried oregano
- 1 teaspoon dried thyme
- ¼ teaspoon freshly ground black pepper
- Toast or crackers for serving

1 In a large bowl, combine the cream cheese, cheddar, and brandy. Beat until smooth. Add the apple, basil, oregano, thyme, and pepper, and stir until completely combined.

2 Spoon the mixture into a crock or small serving dish. Cover and chill for approximately 1 hour. Serve on toast points or crackers.

LOW-FAT OPTIONS

JUST AS LOW-FAT CREAM CHEESE WORKS WELL in this Apple-Cheese Spread, it can be substituted in recipes throughout this book. However, do not substitute fat-free cream cheese; the texture is totally different and it is difficult to blend. You can also use low-fat or reduced-fat mayonnaise, milk, sour cream, and yogurt.

Apples for Good Health

RESEARCHERS IN BRITAIN, FINLAND, FRANCE, AND THE UNITED STATES continue to make new findings relating to the benefits of eating apples and drinking apple juice.

According to a 24-year study by Finland's National Public Health Institute, diets rich in flavonoids, particularly the flavonoid quercetin from apples, are associated with a 46 percent reduced risk of developing cancer. Cornell University researchers reported that apple phytonutrients inhibited the growth of colon and liver cancers in laboratory studies.

Other long-term studies by Finnish researchers found that the quercetin in apples and onions was directly associated with the lowest risk of coronary mortality and that individuals who ate the most apples had the lowest risk of thrombotic stroke.

A 2008 study by the Université Montpellier in France found that apples and apple juice may have cardiovascular protective properties similar to those in grapes and grape juice. Both fruits appear to reduce atherosclerosis, a hardening of the arteries that can lead to stroke or heart attack. The results also suggest that processing the fruit into juice might actually increase the bioavailability of the antioxidant phytonutrients found in whole apples and grapes.

A five-year study conducted by British researchers found that people who eat several apples a week have better lung function than those who don't eat apples. Another recent study concluded that children who drink apple juice daily are not as likely to suffer from breathing problems. Researchers believe that the flavonoids and phenolic acids in apples help relieve asthma symptoms by calming inflammation and improving lung function.

In a University of Massachusetts–Lowell study, researchers concluded that apples and apple juice may protect against Alzheimer's and other age-related illnesses.

A quick and delicious hors d'oeuvre, these wedges also make a wonderful and ever-so-easy first course. Depending on what follows, count on 2 or 3 wedges per person.

PROSCIUTTO APPLE WEDGES

YIELD: 32 wedges

INGREDIENTS

4 medium apples (Red Delicious, Cortland, Empire, Idared), cored and each cut into 8 thin wedges

¼ cup fresh lemon juice

4 ounces cream cheese, softened

8 ounces prosciutto or smoked salmon

1 Brush each cut surface of the apples with lemon juice. Spread the cream cheese thinly on each cut side.

2 Wrap a thin slice of prosciutto around each wedge. Serve immediately or refrigerate. Remove from the refrigerator 30 minutes before serving.

APPLE THOUGHTS

They [apples] must be eaten in the fields, when your system is all aglow with exercise, when the frosty weather nips your fingers, the wind rattles the bare boughs or rustles the few remaining leaves, and the jay is heard screaming around. What is sour in the house a bracing walk makes sweet.

— Henry David Thoreau, from his Journal

CHAPTER 4

Apple Salads & Sides

The crisp, crunchy, tart-sweet flesh of apples can be diced, sliced, or grated and added to just about any salad you may think of making. The understated flavor of apples lends itself to sweet and sour, creamy, garlicky, herbed, and spiced dressings. So when you're short on lettuce, carrots, beets, celery, or any other salad ingredient, slice an apple into your bowl. Apples also go well in many savory side dishes — try mashed baked apples with creamed potatoes, turnips, carrots, and parsnips.

AVOCADO & APPLE COMPOSED SALAD *with*

Buttermilk-Herb Dressing

YIELD: 8–10 side servings or 4 vegetarian mains with the addition of a little cheese

Bantam or small eggs from young chickens (pullets) are ideal in this recipe, but feel free to use regular medium chicken eggs if you can't find bantam or small eggs at your local farmers' market. Be sure to use eggs that are more than a week old. Fresh eggs don't peel easily, and you're likely to lose the first layer of egg white with the shell. With bantam eggs being so small, you would lose too much white, and besides, they would not look very pretty.

1 For the dressing, add the buttermilk, mayonnaise, lemon juice, garlic, mustard, honey, avocado, basil, and salt and pepper to taste to the bowl of a small food processor and process until smooth. Taste and adjust the salt, pepper, and lemon juice as needed. (Leftover dressing will keep in the refrigerator for up to 2 weeks.)

2 Cut the apples into slices and then julienne the slices. In a small bowl, toss the apples with ¼ cup of the buttermilk dressing. Set aside.

3 Cut the tomatoes into quarters, cut the kiwis into half-moon slices, and thinly slice the avocados. Sprinkle lemon juice over the avocado slices or place in a dish and drizzle with a little salad dressing.

4 Place the salad greens on a large platter or in a large serving bowl. Toss with ⅓ cup of the dressing and arrange the apples, tomatoes, kiwi, and avocado over the top. Place the egg halves around the perimeter of the salad. Drizzle a little dressing over the eggs and serve the remaining dressing on the side.

NOTE: To cook the eggs, place them in a medium saucepan, cover with lukewarm water, and bring to a boil over high heat. Turn off the heat and leave in the hot water for 8 minutes for bantam and small eggs or up to 10 minutes for medium. Drain and shake the eggs in the pan to break the shells. Place the cooked eggs in a basin of ice-cold water. Leave on the counter for 30 minutes or refrigerate (in the water) until ready to use. To peel, tap the rounded bottom on the counter and remove the shell beginning at the little air sac. The eggs should peel easily once this end is broken. Rinse under cold water to remove any remaining bits of shell and cut in half lengthwise.

INGREDIENTS

BUTTERMILK-HERB DRESSING

YIELD: 1½–2 cups

- ¾ cup buttermilk
- ¼ cup reduced-fat olive oil mayonnaise, or your favorite mayonnaise
- 2–4 tablespoons fresh lemon juice, to taste
- 4–6 large garlic cloves, to taste
- 1 tablespoon Dijon mustard
- 1 tablespoon honey
- 1 ripe avocado, pitted and peeled
- 1 large handful fresh basil or cilantro leaves and tender stems
- Sea salt and freshly ground black pepper

AVOCADO-APPLE COMPOSED SALAD

- 2 large apples (Honeycrisp, Pink Lady, Red Delicious), cored
- 4–6 medium tomatoes (when out of season I buy red Campari and purple-red Kumato varieties)
- 2–3 ripe kiwis, peeled and cut in half lengthwise
- 2 firm-ripe avocados, cut in half lengthwise, pitted, and peeled
- Squeeze of fresh lemon juice (optional)
- 6–8 cups salad greens, arugula, baby kale, baby spinach, mesclun mix, or any combination
- 12 bantam eggs or 8 medium chicken eggs, hard-boiled, cooled, peeled, and cut in half lengthwise (see note)

Apple Salads & Sides

APPLE, PEAR & BEET COMPOSED SALAD with *Balsamic-Herb Dressing*

YIELD: 4–6 servings

To turn this into a whole-meal salad, I add crumbled cheese — blue, herbed feta, or goat — and a good quantity of nuts. A variety of balsamic glazes is available at most supermarkets. Pomegranate concentrate and pomegranate glaze are available at Middle Eastern and Asian stores if you can't find them at your local supermarket, but you may be surprised at what is showing up on the shelves of upscale grocery stores in response to foodie networks.

1 For the dressing, add the olive oil, vinegar, balsamic glaze, honey, mustard, garlic, basil, mint, tarragon, and salt and pepper to taste to the bowl of a small food processor and process until smooth. Taste and adjust to your liking, if necessary, with a tablespoon or two of water and more salt and pepper. (Leftover dressing will keep in the refrigerator for up to 2 weeks.)

2 In a small bowl, combine the apple and pear slices with 2 tablespoons of the dressing. In another small bowl, toss the beets with 2 tablespoons of the dressing.

3 In a large bowl or wide, deep platter, toss the fennel, olives, and greens with ¼ cup of the dressing.

4 Arrange the beets in the center of the dressed greens and the apple and pear slices around the edges. If desired, sprinkle the cheese and nuts over the salad.

INGREDIENTS

BALSAMIC-HERB DRESSING

YIELD: about 1½ cups

- ¾ cup olive oil
- ¼ cup balsamic vinegar
- 1 tablespoon balsamic glaze or pomegranate concentrate
- 1 tablespoon honey
- 1 tablespoon coarse seeded Maille or Dijon mustard (or 2 tablespoons Dijonnaise)
- 3 large garlic cloves
- ½ cup fresh basil (small handful)
- ¼ cup fresh mint (about 20 leaves)
- 2 tablespoons fresh tarragon
- Sea salt and freshly ground black pepper

APPLE, PEAR, AND BEET COMPOSED SALAD

- 1 medium apple (Pink Lady, Honeycrisp, Gala), peeled if desired, cored, and very thinly sliced
- 1 medium firm pear, peeled if desired, cored, and thinly sliced
- 2 medium beets, peeled and grated (if preferred, cook, peel, and dice or julienne)
- ¼–½ medium fennel bulb, outer layer discarded, hard basal core removed and very thinly sliced or grated on large holes
- ½ cup pitted Kalamata olives, halved lengthwise
- 4–6 cups salad greens, torn or small whole leaves
- 1 cup crumbled blue, feta, or goat cheese (optional)
- 1 cup chopped walnuts or pecans (optional)

I use a "gourmet" salad mix for this, but whenever I can, I harvest the tiny tender greens from my own garden. I also grow lots of arugula (rocket) and spinach, which I can grow and harvest for about 10 months in my Virginia climate.

APPLE & PARMESAN CURL SALAD

YIELD: 4 servings

INGREDIENTS

- ½ cup olive oil
- 2 tablespoons seasoned rice vinegar or balsamic vinegar
- Juice of ½ lime or lemon
- 2 teaspoons Dijon mustard
- 1 garlic clove, minced
- ¼ teaspoon freshly ground black pepper
- Sea salt
- 1 pound baby salad greens, baby spinach, or salad mix
- 2 medium apples (Fuji, Gala, Golden Delicious, Ginger Gold), peeled, cored, cut into halves, and sliced
- ½ cup pine nuts, toasted (see note on page 137)
- 4 ounces Parmesan cheese, shaved into curls

1 In a screw-top jar, combine the oil, vinegar, lime juice, mustard, garlic, pepper, and salt to taste, and shake well.

2 Place the salad greens in a large serving bowl. Add the apples.

3 Shake the vinaigrette again and add 1½ tablespoons to the salad. (Serve the remaining dressing on the side.) Toss the salad, sprinkle with the pine nuts, and top with the Parmesan.

Variation

In place of the Parmesan, toss crumbled feta or blue cheese with the salad greens and apple slices.

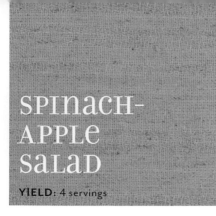

SPINACH-APPLE SALAD

YIELD: 4 servings

If you can use homegrown spinach, it won't need as much washing and rinsing as loose, store-bought bunches. However, if you don't grow your own, you have the option of buying a package of triple-washed spinach. Gritty spinach leaves make for a most unpleasant salad.

1 Place the spinach and lettuce in a salad bowl. Add the apples and toss in the walnuts.

2 In a small bowl, combine the yogurt, honey, coriander, cumin, ginger, and turmeric. Toss with the salad. Serve immediately.

INGREDIENTS

- 4 cups fresh spinach leaves
- 1 small head Boston or Bibb lettuce, leaves torn
- 2 medium apples (Cortland, Granny Smith, Golden Delicious, Braeburn), cored, quartered, and thinly sliced
- ¼ cup chopped walnuts
- ½ cup plain yogurt
- 1 tablespoon honey
- 1 teaspoon ground coriander
- ¼ teaspoon ground cumin
- ¼ teaspoon ground ginger
- ¼ teaspoon ground turmeric

NUTRITIONAL VALUE OF A RAW APPLE

FOR A 2¾-INCH, 138-GRAM RAW APPLE WITH SKIN

Water, 83.93 percent
Calories, 81
Protein, 0.262 gram
Fat, 0.8 gram
Carbohydrates, 21.045 grams
Calcium, 9.66 milligrams
Phosphorus, 9.66 milligrams
Iron, 0.248 milligram

Sodium, 0.00
Potassium, 158.7 milligrams
Vitamin A, 73.14 International Units
Vitamin B$_6$, 0.066 milligram
Thiamine, 0.023 milligram
Riboflavin, 0.019 milligram
Niacin, 0.106 milligram
Vitamin C (ascorbic acid), 7.866 milligrams

Note: There are about 2 large, 3 medium, or 4 small apples in a pound. The USDA Nutrient Database for Standard Reference, Release 13 (November 1999) states that three 2¾-inch apples equal 1 pound.

The absolute classic of apple salads, this traditional recipe is said to have originated at the Waldorf Astoria hotel in New York City sometime in the early 1900s. The basic recipe lends itself to many variations — adding cubes of cooked meat, grilled fish, fresh mozzarella, or marinated tofu will turn it into a satisfying lunch.

waldorf salad

YIELD: 4 servings

INGREDIENTS

- 3 medium apples (Jonagold, Cortland, Braeburn, Empire), peeled, cored, and diced
- 3 stalks celery, diced
- ½ cup chopped walnuts
- ¾ cup heavy cream
- 2 tablespoons fresh lemon juice
- ¼ teaspoon freshly ground white pepper
- 8 fresh mint leaves, torn into small pieces, or 2 tablespoons chopped fresh parsley
- 1 head Boston lettuce, leaves separated

1 Chill a medium bowl for beating the cream.

2 Place the apples in a large bowl. Add the celery and walnuts.

3 In the chilled bowl, beat the cream, lemon juice, and pepper until soft peaks form. Stir into the apple mixture.

4 Sprinkle the mint on top and serve the apple mixture on the lettuce leaves.

KEEP 'EM WHITE

TOSSING APPLES WITH VINAIGRETTE, lemon (citrus) juice, or citric acid powder mixed with water helps keep the flesh from browning. However, some of the up-and-coming apple varieties — particularly Ginger Gold and Cameo — have white flesh that is naturally slow to brown.

APPLE, DRIED FRUIT & ISRAELI COUSCOUS SALAD

YIELD: 6 servings

I also make this grain salad with any variety of rice or a commercial blend of quinoa, couscous, orzo, and baby garbanzo beans. Israeli couscous and the quinoa blend cook in 10 to 12 minutes. The rice, depending on whether it's white, brown, or wild, will require from 20 to 50 minutes.

1   Prepare the couscous according to the package directions, adding ½ teaspoon salt to the cooking water. In a medium bowl, toss the cooked couscous with the 1 tablespoon oil.

2   In a medium serving bowl, whisk together the ¼ cup oil, lemon zest, lemon juice, and salt and pepper to taste. Stir in the apples, scallions, and dried fruits.

3   Add the prepared couscous, almonds, and herbs, and stir to combine.

4   Serve at room temperature. Leftovers can be reheated in the microwave or in a skillet over medium-low heat.

INGREDIENTS

1½ cups toasted Israeli couscous, quinoa blend, or rice

Sea salt

¼ cup plus 1 tablespoon olive oil

Zest of 1 lemon

¼ cup fresh lemon juice

Freshly ground black pepper

2 medium sweet-tart apples (Empire, Cameo, Fuji, Jonagold), peeled if desired, cored, and cut into small dice

4 scallions, white and pale green parts, thinly sliced

½ cup chopped dried apricots, cherries, cranberries, or a combination

½ cup flaked almonds

1 cup snipped fresh herbs, such as mint, parsley, cilantro, or a combination

Farro is an ancient European wheat variety normally purchased in a pearled form that takes about 35 minutes to cook, no presoaking required. Farro is also available semi-pearled and partially cooked, which reduces stove-top time to about 10 minutes. For a gluten-free dish, use buckwheat (kasha) or quinoa; they're both delightful options.

To make this a complete meal for carnivores, add 3 to 4 sausages, cooked without casings and crumbled. Or toss cooked shrimp with the salad at the end.

Farro *with* MUSHROOMS, ONION & APPLE

YIELD: 8 side servings or 4 mains

INGREDIENTS

4–6 large garlic cloves, to taste

1 cup fresh parsley (1 big handful)

2 tablespoons olive oil

1 medium sweet or red onion, diced

1 large apple (Gala, Fuji, Cameo, whatever's on hand but not McIntosh), peeled, cored, and diced

8–12 ounces mushrooms, sliced (use more or less to your liking)

Sea salt and freshly ground black pepper

1½ cups pearled farro (or 2 cups precooked semi-pearled farro), prepared according to package directions

¼ cup apple cider or juice

1 cup chopped walnuts or whole pine nuts, toasted if desired (see note on page 137)

1 cup snipped fresh herbs, such as basil, cilantro, tarragon, or a combination

1 Place the garlic and parsley in the bowl of a food processor and pulse until minced.

2 Heat the oil in a large skillet over medium heat. Add the garlic mixture, onion, and apple, and sauté for 5 minutes. Stir in the mushrooms and salt and pepper to taste and sauté for 10 minutes.

3 Mix in the prepared farro and the cider and cook until the farro is tender and warmed through, 10 to 15 minutes. Stir in the nuts and herbs. Taste and add more salt if necessary.

APPLE-TORTELLINI SALAD

YIELD: 8 servings

For pasta salad lovers, this one from the Michigan Apple Committee is hard to beat. Healthful, with low fat and high fiber, it has lots of flavor, texture, and color. It makes a wonderful addition to a party buffet.

1 For the dressing, in a screw-top jar, combine the apple juice concentrate, agave, vinegar, garlic salt, and pepper to taste, and shake well; refrigerate.

2 For the tortellini salad, cook the tortellini according to the package directions. Drain and cool under cold running water. Shake gently to drain thoroughly.

3 In a large mixing bowl, combine the tortellini, apples, greens, strawberries, celery, and scallions.

4 Toss gently with the chilled dressing. Sprinkle with the pine nuts, if desired, and serve.

INGREDIENTS

DRESSING

- 3 tablespoons thawed frozen apple juice concentrate
- 3 tablespoons agave syrup or honey
- 1 teaspoon cider vinegar
- 1/8 teaspoon garlic salt
- Freshly ground white pepper

TORTELLINI SALAD

- 1 (9-ounce) package refrigerated or frozen cheese-filled tortellini
- 3 medium apples (Empire, Fuji, Braeburn, Gala), peeled, cored, and sliced
- 1 romaine heart or 1/2 head crisp lettuce, shredded, or 2 cups baby spinach or arugula salad greens
- 12 strawberries, hulled and sliced
- 1 tender celery stalk, thinly sliced (about 1/2 cup)
- 3 scallions, white and pale green parts, thinly sliced
- 2 tablespoons toasted pine nuts (optional; see note on page 137)

Don't hesitate to substitute firm tofu for the chicken. Do, however, use the type of tofu packaged in water; I would not use silken firm or even silken extra-firm tofu in a dish that requires tossing since softer-textured tofu breaks apart too easily.

curried chicken salad

YIELD: 4–6 servings

INGREDIENTS

- ⅔ cup sour cream
- ⅓ cup mayonnaise
- 1 tablespoon honey
- 1 tablespoon lime juice
- 2 large garlic cloves, minced
- 1½ teaspoons curry powder
- ½ teaspoon ground cumin
- ½ teaspoon ground ginger
-   Sea salt and freshly ground black pepper
- 2 medium apples (Granny Smith, Northern Spy, Winesap, Braeburn), peeled, cored, and diced
- 4 cups diced cooked chicken
- 2 stalks celery, diced
- ½ cup golden raisins
- 1 head Boston lettuce

1 In a medium bowl, beat together the sour cream, mayonnaise, honey, and lime juice. Add the garlic, curry powder, cumin, ginger, and salt and pepper to taste. Stir until completely combined.

2 Add the apples, chicken, celery, and raisins, and toss to combine.

3 Arrange the lettuce on a serving platter. Spoon the salad onto the bed of lettuce.

ANTIOXIDANT POWERHOUSE

ACCORDING TO RESEARCHERS, 100 grams of unpeeled fresh apple (about two-thirds of a medium apple) provides the antioxidant activity of 1,500 milligrams of vitamin C! Learn more about antioxidants and why apples are good for you in Apples for Good Health (page 64).

POTaTO-
APPLe SaLaD

YIELD: 4–6 servings

Fresh apples add a nice crunch to this potato salad, and they taste wonderful with the smoky-sweet bacon flavor.

1 Put the potatoes in a medium saucepan and cover with cold water. Bring to a boil, cover the pan, and boil gently for approximately 20 minutes, or until they are tender but not falling apart. When cool enough to handle, peel and cut into ½-inch slices.

2 While the potatoes are cooking, fry the bacon in a medium skillet, drain, and chop into ½-inch pieces.

3 Grate the onion into a large bowl.

4 In a small bowl, whisk together the oil, vinegar, and garlic.

5 Add the warm sliced potatoes to the grated onion and toss with the oil mixture. Add the apples and bacon.

6 In a small bowl, stir together the mayonnaise, mustard, and salt and pepper to taste. Add to the salad and toss to combine. Serve at room temperature or chilled.

INGREDIENTS

- 6 medium yellow or red potatoes
- 4 slices bacon, apple-smoked if possible
- 1 medium sweet onion
- ½ cup grapeseed or olive oil
- 2 tablespoons cider vinegar
- 2 garlic cloves, crushed in a garlic press
- 2 medium apples (Cortland, Granny Smith, Jonagold, Fuji), peeled, cored, and diced
- ½ cup mayonnaise
- 1 tablespoon Dijon mustard
- Sea salt and freshly ground black pepper

Apple Salads & Sides

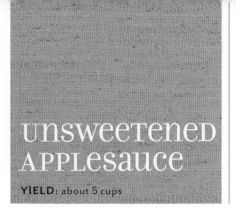

UNSWEETENED APPLESAUCE

YIELD: about 5 cups

Unsweetened applesauce lends itself to any number of savory additions. For example, to serve it with beef, combine ½ cup of freshly grated horseradish and 2 cups of applesauce. If pork or chicken is the main dish, add 2 tablespoons of honey, the grated zest of 1 lime, and ½ teaspoon each of ground ginger and curry powder to 2 cups of applesauce. To accompany duck or goose, flavor 2 cups of applesauce with 2 tablespoons of brandy and 2 tablespoons of honey.

1   Place the apples in a large saucepan with the water and the nutmeg.

2   Cover the pot and cook over low heat for approximately 30 minutes, or until the apples are tender. When cool, crush with a potato masher or purée in a blender or food processor to the desired consistency.

NOTE: For added flavor, leave the peel on and force the cooked apples through a sieve or food mill to separate the skins from the fruit. When puréeing in a blender or food processor, the skins will break down.

INGREDIENTS

10   medium apples (any kind except Red Delicious or summer-harvested apples such as Lodi, Tydeman's Red, and Puritan; blending several types gives the best flavor), peeled, cored, and cut into quarters

1   tablespoon water, apple juice, or fresh lemon juice

½   teaspoon freshly grated or ground nutmeg

This side dish works equally well with torn chard, kale, or mature arugula leaves. Hardy greens will not wilt as quickly as spinach, so you will want to cook them a little longer.

SPINACH *with* LEEK, BACON & APPLE

YIELD: 4 servings

INGREDIENTS

- 4 slices bacon, each cut into ½-inch pieces
- 1 large leek, trimmed, cleaned, and thickly sliced
- Sea salt and freshly ground black pepper
- 2 medium apples, any variety, peeled, cut in half, cored, and cut into small dice or matchsticks
- 1 tablespoon cider vinegar
- 8 cups spinach leaves or torn greens

1 In a large skillet, cook the bacon over medium-high heat until crisp. Remove to a dish and discard most of the bacon fat, leaving just enough to coat the skillet.

2 Add the leek to the skillet and season with salt and pepper to taste. Sauté for 5 minutes. Stir in the apple and cook for 5 minutes. Add the vinegar and spinach and stir to combine. Cover and cook until the spinach has wilted, about 5 minutes.

3 Sprinkle the bacon over the top or stir into the greens and serve hot.

Apple Salads & Sides

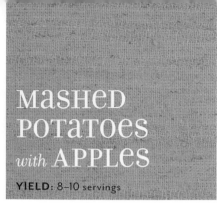

Mashed Potatoes *with* Apples

YIELD: 8–10 servings

I favor yellow potatoes, but white or russet also make fine mashed potatoes. Whatever you usually use are probably already in your pantry. I microwave my potatoes with 1 to 2 tablespoons of water in a 7- by 11-inch glass baking dish covered with plastic wrap. If you want to try this method, for this quantity start with 10 minutes on medium power (7). Test for doneness, then continue with 3- to 5-minute intervals until tender. The potatoes should not be overcooked or crusted on the bottom.

1 Boil or microwave the potatoes, covered, until tender, 15 to 20 minutes. Drain and return to the pan or microwave dish. Add the sour cream, half-and-half, and 2 to 4 tablespoons of the butter to taste. Mash until smooth. Season with the chives and salt and pepper to taste. Keep warm.

2 Heat 2 tablespoons of the remaining butter in a large skillet over medium heat. Add the apples, sprinkle with the nutmeg, and cook, stirring occasionally, until tender and light golden, about 10 minutes. Spoon the apples on top of the mashed potatoes and sprinkle with the cheese, if desired. Serve hot.

INGREDIENTS

- 2 pounds potatoes (4 large), peeled and sliced about ½ inch thick
- ½ cup low-fat or regular sour cream
- ¼ cup half-and-half
- 4–6 tablespoons butter
- 1 tablespoon snipped fresh chives or fresh thyme

  Sea salt and freshly ground black pepper
- 2 medium sweet-tart apples (Fuji, Winesap, Cortland), peeled, cored, and thinly sliced
- ⅛–¼ teaspoon freshly grated or ground nutmeg
- 2 ounces reduced-fat cheddar cheese, grated (optional; about ½ cup)

Apple Salads & Sides

My favorite sweet potatoes have deep-orange flesh. It's not only that I find them more intensely flavored than the pale-golden sweet potatoes; I prefer their dense, smooth texture. Although this purée is a delicious side dish for savory meals, it also makes a good base for a sweet or savory pie filling.

APPLE & SWEET POTATO PURÉE

YIELD: 6 servings

INGREDIENTS

- 2 large sweet potatoes
- 4 tablespoons butter
- 2 large apples (Rome Beauty, Northern Spy, Winesap), peeled, cored, and sliced
- ½ cup heavy cream or sour cream
- ¼ teaspoon sea salt
- ½ teaspoon freshly grated nutmeg or ¼ teaspoon ground
- ¼ teaspoon ground ginger

1 Preheat the oven to 350°F. Grease a rimmed baking sheet.

2 Place the potatoes on the prepared baking sheet and bake for 1½ hours, or until very tender.

3 In a medium skillet, melt the butter over low heat. Add the apples and cook until tender, about 15 minutes. Transfer to a large bowl.

4 Peel the potatoes while still warm and add to the apples. Add the cream, salt, nutmeg, and ginger. Mash together with a fork, then whip the mixture with an electric mixer until the texture is creamy. Serve at once.

UNIVERSITY OF MINNESOTA APPLE-BREEDING PROGRAM

THE UNIVERSITY OF MINNESOTA HAS BEEN BREEDING APPLE VARIETIES since 1878. The Fruit Breeding Farm, now known as the Horticultural Research Center, was created in 1908 on 80 acres near Victoria, Minnesota. This has become a recognized center of fruit research and breeding, particularly for northern climates. Since their breeding program began, they have developed and released 24 apple varieties, including Fireside, Haralson, Honeycrisp, Honeygold, SnowSweet, Sweet 16, SweeTango, and Zestar!.

maple–sweet potato casserole

Though this dish is usually served alongside a savory entrée — the sweet flavors are particularly fine accompaniments to roast meats and stuffing — it also makes a delicious warm or cold sweet dessert served with a whipped-cream topping or sour cream sweetened with brown sugar.

1 Place the potatoes in a pot of boiling water. Cook for 20 minutes, or until easily pierced with a fork. Cool and peel.

2 Preheat the oven to 350°F. Grease a 9- by 13-inch baking pan.

3 Cut the potatoes into ½-inch slices. Arrange a single layer of potatoes in the prepared pan.

4 Toss the apples with the lemon juice. Place a single layer of apples over the potatoes. Continue layering alternately until all the apple and potato slices have been used.

5 In a small saucepan, melt the butter over low heat. Stir in the maple syrup, nutmeg, cinnamon, and salt. Pour over the layers.

6 Bake for 30 minutes, until the apples are tender. Serve hot or warm.

INGREDIENTS

- 6 medium sweet potatoes, scrubbed
- 2 medium apples (Baldwin, Granny Smith, Northern Spy), peeled, cored, and cut into ½-inch slices
- Juice of 1 lemon
- ½ cup (1 stick) butter
- ½ cup maple syrup
- ½ teaspoon freshly grated or ground nutmeg
- ¼ teaspoon ground cinnamon
- ¼ teaspoon sea salt

I love Brussels sprouts. My husband doesn't. They're bitter, he says. So, at Thanksgiving I dress them up with buttery apples slices. I like to oven-roast the sprouts, but if there is no room in the holiday oven, then I pan-roast in a large skillet. Before serving, add color with a sprinkling of dried cranberries.

SPRUCED-UP BRUSSELS SPROUTS

YIELD: 8 servings

INGREDIENTS

- 1 pound Brussels sprouts, old outer leaves discarded, cut in half lengthwise
- 2 medium apples (Gala, Golden Delicious, Pink Lady, Fortune), peeled, cored, and cut into ¼-inch slices
- 1 tablespoon olive oil
- Sea salt and freshly ground black pepper
- 8–10 fresh sage leaves, stacked, cut lengthwise, then cut finely crosswise
- 2 tablespoons butter, cut into small pieces
- ¼ cup dried cranberries

1 Preheat the oven to 400°F or heat a large skillet over medium heat.

2 Place the Brussels sprouts and apples on a baking sheet. Drizzle with the oil and season with salt and pepper to taste. Scatter the sage over the sprouts, then, using your hands, toss to mix well.

3 If oven-roasting, dot with the butter and roast for about 20 minutes, or until done to your liking. If pan-roasting, slide the tossed Brussels sprouts and apples into the heated skillet. Dot with the butter and cook for 20 minutes, stirring occasionally. Don't stir too often or they will become mushy and fail to caramelize. Serve hot with dried cranberries sprinkled on top.

Apple Salads & Sides

APPLE RATATOUILLE

YIELD: 8 servings

I learned to make ratatouille when living as a student in Geneva, Switzerland. My roommate would make a huge pot and we would feast on it for days. Sometimes we had it over rice, other times over noodles. When we were tired of eating it hot, we layered it on thick slices of bread, sprinkled it with a little cheese, and heated it in the oven. The apple in this version is an interesting variation on the usual eggplant.

1 Heat the oil in a large skillet over medium heat and add the onion. With a garlic press, crush the garlic directly into the skillet and sauté for 5 minutes.

2 Season with the oregano, allspice, and salt and pepper to taste. Stir in the bell peppers and sauté for 10 minutes.

3 Add the zucchini and tomatoes. Stir, cover, and cook over low heat for 20 minutes.

4 Add the apples and cook, covered, 15 minutes longer. Serve hot.

INGREDIENTS

2 tablespoons olive oil

1 large onion, sliced

4 large garlic cloves

2 teaspoons dried oregano

½ teaspoon ground allspice

Sea salt and freshly ground black pepper

2 green bell peppers, seeds and ribs removed, sliced

2 medium zucchini, sliced

6 ripe medium tomatoes, cut into quarters

2 medium apples (Rome Beauty, Granny Smith, Northern Spy), peeled, cored, and diced

acorn SQUASH *with* RICE, APPLE & PECAN STUFFING

YIELD: 4 servings

Acorn squash, or any winter squash, takes a long time to cook in the oven, so I start mine off in the microwave. My favorite squash is butternut, but acorn and Delicata have deeper cavities, perfect for filling with this savory stuffing.

INGREDIENTS

- 2 acorn or Delicata squash, pricked a few times on both sides with a fork
- 1 cup cooked rice or cooked barley
- 1 large apple (Cameo, Jonamac, Rome), peeled, cored, and cut into small dice
- 1/4 cup chopped pecans or walnuts
- Sea salt and freshly ground black pepper
- 1/2 teaspoon ground cinnamon
- 1/2 teaspoon ground cumin, or to taste
- 4 ounces crumbled herbed feta cheese (1 cup)

1 Preheat the oven to 400°F. Grease a 9- by 13-inch baking dish.

2 Place 1 whole squash in a 7- by 11-inch microwave-safe dish. Cover with a paper towel and microwave on high for 4 minutes. Turn and microwave another 4 minutes. Remove and let stand, uncovered, for 5 to 10 minutes before cutting the squash in half. Scoop out and discard the seeds (or feed them to chickens). Repeat with the second squash.

3 While the squash are cooling, combine the rice, apple, pecans, salt and pepper to taste, cinnamon, and cumin in a microwave-safe dish. Microwave on high for 1½ minutes. Remove and stir in half of the feta.

4 Place the seeded squash halves cut side up in the prepared baking dish. Spoon one-quarter of the filling into each cavity and roast for 15 to 20 minutes, or until the squash are perfectly tender and the filling is hot.

5 Sprinkle with the remaining feta and broil for 2 minutes, or until the cheese has melted.

RICE-STUFFED APPLES

YIELD: 4 servings

Make a quick variation of this dish by using leftover cooked rice (jasmine is wonderful) and cooking the apples in the microwave on high for 3 to 4 minutes per apple. Serve as a side dish or for a light lunch.

1 Preheat the oven to 350°F.

2 In a medium skillet, melt 2 tablespoons of the butter over medium heat. Add the onion and sauté for 5 minutes.

3 Stir in the water, rice, allspice, ginger, and salt and pepper to taste. Bring to a boil over high heat, reduce the heat, and cook, covered, over low heat for 20 minutes, or until the rice is tender but not soft. Stir in the raisins.

4 Core the apples, leaving about ¼ inch of flesh at the base. Scoop out approximately ¼ inch of flesh from the centers; chop and add to the rice mixture.

5 Place the apples in a 7- by 9-inch baking dish and spoon the rice stuffing into and on top of the apples. Pour the apple juice over the top.

6 Cut the remaining 1 tablespoon butter into small pieces and dot over the stuffed apples. Cover the dish loosely with aluminum foil.

7 Bake for 45 minutes. Serve hot as a side dish with roast chicken or pork.

INGREDIENTS

- 3 tablespoons butter
- 1 medium onion, chopped
- 1¼ cups water
- ½ cup uncooked rice
- ½ teaspoon ground allspice
- ½ teaspoon ground ginger
- Sea salt and freshly ground black pepper
- ½ cup raisins
- 4 large apples (Rome Beauty, Mutsu/Crispin, Winesap)
- ¼ cup apple juice or cider

APPLe KeBaBS

Stringing apple wedges on skewers makes them easy to broil. They taste delicious with ham or chicken. These kebabs are also fun as a snack or for dessert; drizzle them with a little chocolate sauce for added sweetness.

YIELD: 6 servings

INGREDIENTS

- 6 medium apples (Gala, Braeburn, Honeycrisp, Golden Delicious)
- 4 tablespoons butter
- 1 tablespoon creamy peanut butter
- ½ teaspoon ground cinnamon
- ½ teaspoon ground ginger
- ½ teaspoon freshly grated or ground nutmeg

1 Peel, core, and cut each apple into 6 wedges. Cut each wedge in half. Thread the apple pieces on six skewers and place on a broiling pan.

2 In a small skillet, melt the butter. Add the peanut butter, cinnamon, ginger, and nutmeg, and stir until combined and heated through.

3 Brush the apple chunks with the mixture and broil for 4 minutes (1 minute per side). Baste generously each time the skewers are given a quarter turn. Serve hot.

SPECIAL EQUIPMENT

IF YOU'RE PEELING, CORING, AND SLICING apples in quantity, you might find it useful to acquire an apple peeler that also cores. I use a Colonial (old-fashioned) type of corer and a small paring knife to peel my apples, but there are several hand-cranked and electric peelers, corers, and slicers available in stores and online. These are a boon to anyone who has bushels of apples to process or bake into pies.

APPLe, sausaGe & CHeese straTa

YIELD: 10–12 side servings or 6 mains

Use any thick-cut sliced bread for this baked dish. If the bread is very fresh, let the cubes sit out on a baking tray to dry. For the cheese, choose grated cheddar, mixed Mexican-style, or odds and ends on hand, even crumbled blue or feta. Mozzarella is not a good choice because it forms strands rather than melting into the layers. A strata like this can serve as a festive dinner or brunch side, or as a main dish with a salad or roasted vegetable.

1   Preheat the oven to 350°F. Grease a 9- by 13-inch baking dish.

2   Heat a large skillet over medium heat. Crumble in the sausages and cook, stirring occasionally, for 10 minutes. Stir in the onion and fennel and cook for 5 minutes. Add the apples, fennel fronds, and salt and pepper to taste, and cook, stirring occasionally, for 5 minutes. Remove from the heat.

3   Spread half of the bread pieces in the prepared baking dish. Cover with half of the sausage mixture. Sprinkle half of the cheese over the top. Make another layer with the bread and top with the remaining sausage mixture.

4   In a large bowl, beat the eggs, then whisk in the milk. Pour over the bread and sausage mixture. Using the back of a serving spoon or a spatula, lightly press down on the strata. Sprinkle the remaining 1 cup cheese over the top. Let the strata sit at room temperature for 15 minutes so the bread can begin to soak up the liquids.

5   Bake for 45 to 50 minutes, until puffed and golden.

6   Serve warm or at room temperature.

INGREDIENTS

4   sweet Italian sausages, casings removed

1   medium sweet onion, diced

¼   medium fennel bulb, tough outer layers and basal core removed, grated on large holes of box grater, or more to taste

2   medium apples (ripe Granny Smith, Stayman, Fuji), peeled, cored, and diced

2   tablespoons snipped fresh fennel fronds or chopped fresh rosemary or fresh thyme

Sea salt and freshly ground black pepper

1   loaf Italian or French (soft-crust) bread, cut into ½-inch slices, then 1-inch pieces (5–6 cups)

2   cups grated or crumbled cheese of choice (except mozzarella)

4   large eggs

3   cups whole or low-fat milk

APPLE & RED BELL PEPPER STUFFING BALLS

YIELD: 4 servings

Doesn't everybody love stuffing? Here is a novel way to present it — not actually stuffed into the roast but baked alongside in generous mounds.

1 Heat the oil in a large skillet over medium heat and sauté the apple, bell peppers, onion, and garlic for 10 minutes. Remove from the heat.

2 Add the bread to the skillet with the apple juice, thyme, mace, and salt and pepper to taste.

3 Add the egg and stir to completely combine.

4 Form the stuffing into 4 balls and arrange around a pork or poultry roast to cook for the last 45 minutes of roasting time.

INGREDIENTS

2 tablespoons olive oil

1 medium apple (Granny Smith, Braeburn, Idared), peeled, cored, and chopped

2 red bell peppers, seeds and ribs removed, chopped

1 medium red onion, chopped

1 garlic clove, minced

6 slices whole-wheat bread, cut into cubes

¼ cup apple juice or cider

1 teaspoon dried thyme or 1 tablespoon fresh

½ teaspoon ground mace

Sea salt and freshly ground black pepper

1 egg, beaten

Mild, sweet Italian sausages add good flavor to this stuffing. Simply skin them and crumble them into the skillet. You might also want to substitute sweet onions for the red ones.

sausage & APPLE STUFFING

YIELD: stuffing for a 10- to 12-pound turkey

INGREDIENTS

½ pound sweet Italian pork sausage, casings removed

1 medium apple (Idared, Empire, Golden Delicious, Granny Smith), peeled, cored, and chopped

2 medium red onions, chopped

½ teaspoon ground ginger

½ teaspoon ground mace

½ teaspoon dried sage or 1 tablespoon chopped fresh

½ teaspoon dried thyme or 1 tablespoon fresh

Sea salt and freshly ground black pepper

8 slices whole-wheat bread, torn into small pieces

1 egg, beaten

1 In a large skillet, cook the sausage for 5 minutes over medium heat, breaking it up with a spoon as it cooks.

2 Add the apple, onions, ginger, mace, sage, thyme, and salt and pepper to taste, and sauté for 5 minutes.

3 Add the bread and egg and stir to completely combine.

4 Stuff into a 10- to 12-pound turkey and bake. The stuffing can also be baked separately in a greased 1½-quart baking dish for 45 minutes at 350°F.

Apple Salads & Sides

corn bread–APPLE STUFFING

Make your own corn bread or muffins from scratch (or from a mix) the day before so you can enjoy them fresh for dinner, then use the leftovers in the stuffing the following day.

1 Heat the oil in a medium skillet over medium heat. Add the celery and onion and sauté for 5 minutes.

2 Add the parsley, oregano, and apples, and sauté for 5 minutes. Stir in the corn bread.

3 In a small bowl, beat together the apple juice and egg. Mix into the stuffing.

4 Stuff into a 5- to 6-pound chicken and bake. The stuffing can also be baked separately in a greased 1-quart baking dish for 45 minutes at 350°F.

INGREDIENTS

- 2 tablespoons olive oil or butter
- 2 stalks celery, chopped
- 1 medium red onion, chopped
- ¼ cup chopped fresh parsley
- 1 teaspoon dried oregano
- 2 medium apples (Empire, Idared, Golden Delicious), peeled, cored, and chopped
- 2 cups crumbled corn bread (2 large muffins or 4 slices of bread)
- ¼ cup apple juice
- 1 egg

ADD AN APPLE

AMONG MY FAVORITE APPLE SIDE DISHES are apple-based stuffings. An apple can be added to almost any stuffing recipe without throwing it off balance; it will impart only a mild flavor, but it will make the stuffing a little moister. Use ¼ cup apple juice to replace some water or broth in your stuffing — it will make the dressing a touch sweeter.

POTATO & APPLE LATKES

YIELD: 20–24 latkes

Traditional potato pancakes serve as a regular side dish for Hanukkah (usually without the addition of apple), but they make a wonderful accompaniment to many meals. Because the grated raw potatoes weep before cooking, I grate them in a food processor right before they are ready to go into the skillet. Even so, it's still good to press the grated vegetables in a colander to remove as much liquid as possible.

1 Fit a food processor with the large-holed shredding disk and process the potatoes, onion, and apple.

2 Remove the mixture to a colander and press out as much liquid as possible by squeezing with your hands. (Alternatively, put the grated mixture into a tea towel and squeeze out the liquid over the sink.)

3 Place the mixture in a large bowl and stir in the egg, flour, herbs, and salt and pepper to taste.

4 Preheat the oven to 250°F and line a baking sheet with paper towels. As each batch of latkes is done, you will want to keep them warm in the oven.

5 Heat 2 to 3 tablespoons of oil in a large skillet over medium heat. When the pan is very hot, scoop up ¼ cup of the potato mixture and add to the pan. Repeat until you have 5 or 6 latkes in the skillet. Leave enough room between the scoops to flatten each latke into a ½-inch-thick pancake. Cook until golden and crisp, about 4 minutes per side. Use a slotted spatula to transfer to the paper towel–lined baking sheet and put in the oven to stay warm.

6 Repeat using the same procedure for the rest of the potato mixture, adding the latkes to the baking sheet to keep warm as each batch is done.

7 Serve warm with the applesauce and sour cream on the side.

INGREDIENTS

4 large baking potatoes. peeled and cut into chunks to fit into a food processor's feed chute

1 medium sweet or red onion, cut into chunks to fit into a food processor's feed chute

1 medium apple (Rome, Ginger Gold, Granny Smith, not too juicy), peeled, cored, and cut into chunks to fit into a food processor's feed chute

1 large egg, beaten

¼ cup all-purpose flour or matzo meal

1 tablespoon chopped fresh herbs, such as fennel, dill, or parsley

Sea salt and freshly ground black pepper

Canola or grapeseed oil for frying

Unsweetened Applesauce (page 80) and sour cream for serving

Apple Salads & Sides

This can also be turned into a salsa to serve with turkey-stuffed flour tortillas. Spice it up by adding extra chopped onion and a minced jalapeño or other hot pepper. All the chopping for this recipe is done in the same food processor bowl — quick and easy — but it does have to sit for a day or two before eating.

SPICY CRANBERRY-APPLE RELISH

YIELD: 4 cups

INGREDIENTS

- 2 medium apples (Granny Smith, Empire, Braeburn), peeled, cored, and each cut into roughly 8 pieces
- 1 orange
- ½ cup sugar
- 2 cups fresh cranberries
- 1 small sweet onion, cut into quarters
- 2 tablespoons fresh lemon juice
- 1 tablespoon brandy
- 1 teaspoon ground ginger
- ¼ teaspoon cayenne pepper
- ¼ teaspoon ground cloves

1 Process the apples in a food processor until coarsely chopped. Transfer to a medium bowl.

2 Remove the zest of the orange in thin strips, being careful not to include the white pith. Process the zest with the sugar until finely chopped. Transfer to the bowl with the apples. Squeeze in the juice of the orange.

3 Process the cranberries, 1 cup at a time, until coarsely chopped. Add to the apple mixture.

4 Process the onion until coarsely chopped. Add to the apple mixture along with the lemon juice, brandy, ginger, cayenne, and cloves, and stir.

5 Cover the bowl and refrigerate for a day or two before serving.

Fall Fruit Relish

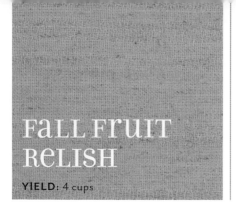

YIELD: 4 cups

Tart cranberries are mellowed with the natural sweetness of apples and pears for a fine condiment for roasts or poultry. If you prefer an even sweeter relish, dissolve 2 tablespoons of honey or maple syrup in the apple juice.

In a large bowl, combine the apples, pears, cranberries, dates, nuts, apple juice, orange zest, cinnamon, and cloves; cover and refrigerate. Leftover relish can be stored in a covered jar in the refrigerator for up to 2 weeks.

INGREDIENTS

- 2 medium sweet apples (Golden Delicious, Gala, Honeycrisp), peeled, cored, and finely chopped
- 2 medium pears, peeled, cored, and chopped
- ¾ cup fresh cranberries, coarsely chopped
- ½ cup chopped pitted dates
- ½ cup chopped walnuts or pecans, toasted (see note on page 137)
- ½ cup apple juice
- 1 teaspoon grated orange zest
- ½ teaspoon ground cinnamon
- ⅛ teaspoon ground cloves

Apple Salads & Sides

Pick Your Own Apples

A WONDERFUL WAY TO CELEBRATE THE AUTUMN HARVEST is to take friends and family on a picnic to a local orchard and spend the day picking your own apples. Some pick-your-own orchards also provide diversions that include warm apple cider and hot doughnuts, pumpkin patches, and hayrides. Most kids, however, find it a special enough experience to wander through avenues of trees and pluck apples right off the branches or find deliciously ripe ones that have fallen to the ground. Adults can take pleasure in discovering heirloom varieties that are not widely cultivated and rarely available except at the orchards and local farm stands or farmers' markets.

When you're picking apples in orchards that were planted decades ago, chances are the trees will be large, with the biggest and ripest apples growing on the highest branches in full sun. To help you reach those high-growing beauties, some orchards may provide ladders or telescopic picking poles with attached baskets.

In more recently established orchards, most of the large, high-canopied apple trees of old have been replaced with high-yielding semidwarf and dwarf tree varieties, which bear an abundance of apples on branches that can be reached by adults of medium height.

When to Pick

Though the main apple harvest falls between mid-October and November, some apple varieties, such as Jonagold, Stayman, Empire, Jonathan, and Golden and Red Delicious, are often ready for harvesting in northern states in late September or early October. Early October to Halloween is usually peak picking time for heirloom varieties such as Black Twig, Esopus Spitzenburg, and Ashmead's Kernel.

Where to Pick

To find out where and when to visit pick-your-own orchards in your area, contact the local County Agricultural Extension Office, visitor and tourist center, or chamber of commerce. You'll also discover that some orchards host fall festivals. For apple-picking tips, see page 138.

CHAPTER 5

Apples Make the Meal

Applesauce in meat loaf — it makes a very moist and tasty one. Grated, sliced, or cubed, apples add another dimension to soups, meat pies, poultry, pork, beef, and lamb. In fact, is there any meat dish that can't take apples? Whether you are preparing a casual supper or a formal dinner, apples belong on the menu.

butternut squash & apple soup

YIELD: 6 servings

Substitute carrots, beets, or pumpkin pound for pound for the butternut squash to create several variations on this classic soup. In general, butternuts weigh in at around 1½ pounds and lose ¼ pound when peeled and seeded. To turn this into a hearty main dish, add 2 to 4 cups cooked garbanzo beans or 2 to 4 chicken thighs, cooked, boned, and cut into bite-size chunks.

Apples Make the Meal

1 Preheat the oven to 400°F.

2 Place the squash, onion, apples, and garlic on a large baking sheet or roasting pan. Sprinkle with salt and pepper to taste, cinnamon, cumin, and curry powder. Drizzle with the oil and stir to combine. Roast for 30 minutes.

3 Spoon the roasted vegetables into a soup pot placed over medium heat. Pour in the broth and cider. If the liquid does not cover the vegetables, add a little water or more cider. Bring to a boil over high heat, then reduce the heat to low and simmer, covered, for 15 minutes.

4 Using an immersion blender, purée the vegetables until smooth, or use a slotted spoon to remove the vegetables to a food processor or blender and purée several cups at a time. Return the purée to the pot.

5 Stir the half-and-half and cilantro into the soup. Taste and adjust with additional salt and pepper or cumin and curry, if desired. Sprinkle each serving with the toasted seeds.

INGREDIENTS

- 1½ pounds butternut squash, peeled, seeded, and cut into 1-inch chunks (4–5 cups)
- 1 medium red onion, sliced
- 2 medium sweet-tart apples (Braeburn, Gala, Fuji), peeled, cored, and sliced or coarsely chopped
- 4 large garlic cloves, sliced
- Sea salt and freshly ground black pepper
- ½ teaspoon ground cinnamon
- ½ teaspoon ground cumin
- ½ teaspoon curry powder
- 2 tablespoons olive oil
- 4 cups chicken or vegetable broth
- 1 cup apple cider
- 1 cup half-and-half
- ½ cup snipped fresh cilantro
- ½ cup toasted sunflower or pumpkin seeds

Whether served hot or at room temperature, this starter comes together very fast and can be made while the rest of the dinner is cooking. Or serve it at lunch accompanied by crusty bread and an olive tapenade.

ZUCCHINI & APPLE SOUP

YIELD: 4–6 servings

INGREDIENTS

- 2 tablespoons butter
- 1 tablespoon olive oil
- 1 large apple (Rome Beauty, Northern Spy, Winesap), peeled, cored, and diced
- 2 medium zucchini, chopped
- 1 large red onion, sliced
- 4 large garlic cloves, minced
- ½ cup hard apple cider or semi-dry sherry
- ½ teaspoon freshly grated nutmeg
- ½ teaspoon freshly ground black pepper
- Sea salt
- 4 cups chicken or vegetable broth
- ½ cup light cream
- ½ cup chopped fresh parsley
- Freshly grated nutmeg for serving (optional)

1   Heat the butter and oil in a soup pot over medium heat. Add the apple, zucchini, onion, and garlic, and sauté for 5 to 10 minutes, or until soft.

2   Add the cider, nutmeg, pepper, and salt to taste. Reduce the heat to low, cover the pan, and simmer 15 minutes longer.

3   Add the broth, cover the pan, and continue cooking 5 minutes longer.

4   Purée the vegetables in a blender or food processor (or force through a sieve). Return the vegetables to the pot, add the cream, and bring to a fast boil over high heat.

5   Pour into serving bowls and sprinkle with the parsley; dust with additional pepper and a little nutmeg, if desired.

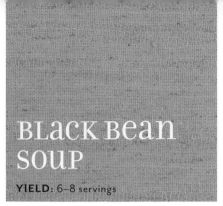

BLACK BEAN SOUP

YIELD: 6–8 servings

Make this with canned beans, rinsed to remove the salt, and cut your preparation time down to 15 minutes and the cooking time to 30 minutes. Serve the soup over brown or white rice for a heartier meal.

1 Pick over and thoroughly rinse the beans. Place in a large pot, add the water, and bring to a boil over high heat. Remove from the heat, cover the pot, and set aside to soak for 1 hour.

2 Heat the oil in a large Dutch oven over medium heat and sauté the garlic, celery, and onion for 5 minutes.

3 Drain the beans and add to the pot. Stir in the broth, sherry, allspice, cumin, and bay leaf. Bring to a boil over high heat, reduce the heat to low, and simmer, covered, for 2 to 4 hours, depending on how tender you like the beans.

4 Add the apples and sausage during the last 30 minutes of cooking. Season with salt and pepper to taste and serve hot.

INGREDIENTS

- 1 pound dried black beans (turtle beans)
- 6 cups water
- 2 tablespoons olive oil
- 4 large garlic cloves, chopped
- 2 large stalks celery, chopped
- 1 large red onion, chopped
- 3½ cups beef, chicken, or vegetable broth
- ½ cup semi-sweet sherry
- 2 teaspoons ground allspice
- 1 teaspoon ground cumin or curry powder
- 1 bay leaf
- 2 medium tart apples (Granny Smith, Jonagold, Winesap, Idared), peeled, cored, and diced
- 8 ounces sweet Italian sausage links, cut into 2-inch pieces
- 8 ounces hot Italian sausage links, cut into 2-inch pieces
- Sea salt and freshly ground black pepper

Apples Make the Meal

This is a takeoff on Welsh rarebit, which is often made with beer and rarely with apples. My mother used to serve rarebit regularly for a school-day breakfast or a Saturday high tea. She made ours with milk, however, never beer.

INGREDIENTS

- 12 ounces cheddar cheese
- 1 tablespoon butter
- 1 large apple (Rome Beauty, Winesap, Fuji), peeled and cored
- ½ cup light cream
- 1 teaspoon dry mustard
- ½ teaspoon freshly grated nutmeg
- 4 slices buttered toast

1 Grate the cheddar into a medium saucepan. Add the butter. Grate the apple into the pan. Add the cream, mustard, and nutmeg.

2 Cook over low heat, stirring, until all the ingredients are blended.

3 When the mixture begins to bubble, pour over buttered toast and serve.

SEVEN A DAY

THE MEDICAL PROFESSION, HEALTH INSTITUTES, and the Departments of Agriculture and Health and Human Services recommend that we eat at least five to seven servings of fruits and vegetables each day, and that nine is better. But what is a serving? Nine servings means consuming 2 cups of fruit and 2½ cups of vegetables daily. Each of the following apple measurements can be counted as one daily serving of fruit:

❋ One medium apple (how easy it is to munch on an apple and then eat two a day)

❋ 8 ounces of 100 percent pure apple juice (not "cocktail" juice, juice "beverages," or "drinks," which are often diluted and contain sugar or syrup)

❋ ½ cup of applesauce

For the "Nutrition Facts" labeling purposes, the Food and Drug Administration defines a serving size of juice as 8 ounces. The American Dietetic Association defines a serving size of juice as 6 ounces.

BAKED APPLES & CHEESE

YIELD: 6 servings

What a wonderful combination — freshly grated cheddar cheese and apples, good enough to eat between two pieces of whole-grain bread. The leeks add a winning quality to this custard dish. Served hot, warm, or cold, it's a good choice for a light main meal or for a brunch buffet.

1 Preheat the oven to 350°F.

2 Wash the leek and discard the outer layer and any of the tougher green leaves. Cut into ¼-inch slices.

3 Melt the butter in a medium skillet over medium heat, add the leek, and sauté for 5 minutes. Transfer to an 8-inch square baking dish.

4 Layer the apple slices over the leek and sprinkle with the cheddar.

5 In a medium bowl, beat together the half-and-half, eggs, curry paste, and salt and pepper to taste. Pour over the cheddar.

6 Bake for 40 to 45 minutes, or until the custard is set and a knife inserted into the center comes out clean.

INGREDIENTS

1   large leek

2   tablespoons butter

3   cups Canned Apple Slices (page 208), drained

4   ounces cheddar cheese, grated (1 cup)

1½ cups half-and-half or light cream

3   eggs

1   teaspoon mild curry paste or powder

Sea salt and freshly ground black pepper

I often make a wrap for a quick and easy lunch. The flour tortillas are lighter than the two slices of bread I'd use to make a sandwich, and the filling is lean and healthful.

TUNA-APPLE TORTILLA WRAPS

YIELD: 2 wraps

INGREDIENTS

- 2 (8-inch) flour tortillas
- 2 tablespoons spread, such as herbed cream cheese, puréed roasted peppers, hummus, or baba ghanoush
- 1 large apple (Nittany, Gala, Braeburn, Golden Delicious), peeled, cored, and thinly sliced
- 1 (6½-ounce) can solid white tuna in water or oil, drained
- 1 tablespoon reduced-fat mayonnaise or sour cream
- Sea salt and freshly ground black pepper
- Mild curry powder for sprinkling (optional)
- 2 scallions, white and green parts, cut in half crosswise, then cut in half lengthwise

1 Place the tortillas on dinner plates and spread each with 1 tablespoon of the spread of your choice. Arrange the apple slices down the center of the tortillas, staying well within 1 inch from the front and back edges.

2 In a small bowl, flake the tuna and combine with the mayonnaise and salt and pepper to taste. Spoon the tuna mixture over the apple slices. Sprinkle with a dash of curry powder, if desired. Top with the scallions.

3 Roll the wraps from front to back and serve immediately. To take along in a lunch box or brown bag, wrap securely in plastic wrap or place in a resealable plastic bag.

Variation

You can also fill the wraps with leftover grilled fresh tuna or salmon, turkey or chicken breast, or smoked salmon. The flavor of apple also goes well with the fresh mozzarella I buy at the supermarket or from a dairy just outside Leesburg, Virginia.

Apples Make the Meal

GRILLED TUNA
with APPLE CHUTNEY

YIELD: 8 servings

My friend Ivan Lillie, a caterer and private chef, has served me some pretty wonderful meals. Of the many recipes I've borrowed from him, this is one of my favorites.

1 Place the tuna steaks in a single layer in a large dish. For the marinade, in a large bowl, combine the cider vinegar, rice wine vinegar, ginger, garlic, brown sugar, and salt and pepper to taste, and stir well. Pour the marinade over the tuna and leave at room temperature for about 30 minutes, turning the tuna in the marinade once or twice.

2 To make the chutney, wearing rubber gloves, seed and mince the peppers. Combine the peppers, apples, onion, garlic, vinegar, and brown sugar in a medium saucepan set over low heat and simmer, stirring occasionally, for about 20 minutes, or until the apples are tender.

3 Remove the tuna from the dish, pour off and discard the marinade, and return the tuna to the dish. In a small bowl, whisk together the olive and sesame oils; drizzle over the tuna. Turn the steaks to coat both sides.

4 Heat a grill to high and position the racks 4 inches from the heat. Grill the tuna steaks for 2 to 3 minutes on each side for rare (3 to 4 minutes for medium rare).

5 Serve each steak with a generous spoonful of the chutney.

INGREDIENTS

- 8 tuna steaks (1 inch thick, or about 6 ounces each)
- ½ cup cider vinegar
- ½ cup seasoned rice wine vinegar
- 6 large chunks crystallized ginger, chopped
- 4 garlic cloves, minced
- 1 tablespoon firmly packed brown sugar

  Salt and freshly ground black pepper
- 2 tablespoons olive oil
- 1 tablespoon toasted sesame oil

APPLE CHUTNEY

- 2 jalapeño peppers
- 4 medium apples (Idared, York, Stayman, Braeburn), peeled, cored, and diced
- 1 medium white onion, diced
- 6 large garlic cloves, chopped
- ½ cup cider vinegar
- ½ cup firmly packed brown sugar

BROILED FISH with APPLE-COCONUT CRUST

YIELD: 6 servings

I love to use cilantro or cinnamon basil in this dish, but any light, fresh herb you prefer can be used. If opting for tarragon, start with ¼ cup leaves and work up from there.

I find that fresh coconut (an unopened new package or flesh fresh from the shell) will process into a relatively smooth texture for the purée. Coconut from an opened package that has been stored in the freezer or refrigerator will have a drier texture and will benefit from presoaking in the coconut milk. A 2-cup Ninja mini processor/blender with a multilayered blade makes wonderfully smooth purées.

1   For the apple purée, combine the apple, garlic, coconut milk, coconut, lemon juice, cilantro, and salt and pepper to taste in a food processor and process until smooth.

2   Make 6 puddles of purée, about 1 tablespoon each, on a baking sheet. Place the fish fillets on top of the purée, then spoon more purée over the fillets to create a light crust. You should have some purée left. Set it aside for serving. At this point, you can refrigerate the fish for an hour or so until ready to cook.

3   Preheat the broiler. Position the fish 5 to 6 inches from the heat source and broil for 6 to 10 minutes, or until the crust is nicely golden and bubbling and the fish flakes when tested with a fork in the center of a fillet.

4   Serve hot with additional coconut purée on the side.

NOTE: Flounder or trout fillets will take about 6 minutes to cook under the broiler. Salmon and thicker white fish, such as cod and tilapia, will take 8 to 10 minutes.

INGREDIENTS

1 medium apple (McIntosh, Empire, Gala), peeled, cored, and cut into 1-inch chunks

2 large garlic cloves

¾ cup low-fat coconut milk

½ cup sweetened shredded coconut (if not using sweetened, add 1 teaspoon honey)

2 teaspoons fresh lemon or lime juice

1 large handful fresh cilantro, basil, or dill (tough stems removed), or more to taste

Sea salt and freshly ground black pepper (¼–½ teaspoon each)

6 fillets cod, hake, or other white fish, or salmon (about 1½ pounds total)

The large, solid flakes of cod make it an ideal choice for this dish. However, you may want to substitute scallops, shrimp, or monkfish. I usually use a mild curry for this dish, but there's no reason not to use a spicy one if that is more to your taste.

CODFISH & APPLE CURRY

YIELD: 4 servings

INGREDIENTS

- 1 tablespoon olive oil
- 1 large red or sweet onion, chopped
- 2 garlic cloves, minced
- 2 medium apples (Golden Delicious, Empire, Honeycrisp, Ginger Gold), peeled, cored, and chopped
- 1 (28-ounce) can crushed tomatoes
- ¼ cup raisins
- 2 tablespoons chutney
- 2 teaspoons curry powder (or to taste)
- Sea salt and freshly ground black pepper
- 1½ pounds cod steaks, skin and bones removed, cut into 1½- to 2-inch pieces
- Cooked rice for serving

1 Heat the oil in a large skillet over medium heat and sauté the onion and garlic for 10 minutes.

2 Stir in the apples, tomatoes, raisins, chutney, curry powder, and salt and pepper to taste, and cook for 15 to 20 minutes, or until the onions and apples are tender.

3 Stir in the cod and cook for 5 to 10 minutes, or just until tender. Serve over rice, if desired.

sea scallops with coriander & cider sauce

YIELD: 6 servings

This is a recipe from Patty Power, co-owner with her husband, Rob Miller, of Distillery Lane Ciderworks (DLC) in Jefferson, Maryland. Patty and Rob produce fresh and bottled hard cider from a variety of heirloom and modern-day apples. Patty uses DLC's The Jefferson hard cider in this recipe. (See profile on page 117.)

1 In a small bowl, combine the coriander, salt, pepper, and nutmeg. Set aside 1 teaspoon of this mix for sprinkling over the finished dish.

2 Place the scallops on paper towels and blot dry. Coat each flat side with the seasoning mixture and set the coated scallops aside.

3 Heat 1 tablespoon of the oil in a small skillet over medium heat and sauté the leek until soft but not browned, about 5 minutes. Set aside.

4 Add the stock, sweet and hard ciders, ginger, coriander seeds, thyme, and lemon zest to a medium saucepan set over medium heat. Bring to a slow boil and cook until reduced to 1½ cups. Strain the sauce, return it to the saucepan, and set aside.

5 Heat the remaining 2 tablespoons oil in a large skillet over medium-high heat. Add half the seasoned scallops and cook 3 minutes on each side. Remove to a plate and tent with foil to keep warm while cooking the remaining scallops, adding a drop more oil as necessary.

6 Return the sauce to a boil and, using a wire whisk, whip in the butter to create a smooth emulsion. Divide the sauce among six plates. Spoon equal amounts of the warm leek slices over the sauce and arrange five scallops on the side of each plate. Sprinkle the scallops with the reserved seasoning mixture and serve immediately.

INGREDIENTS

- 4 tablespoons ground coriander
- 1 teaspoon salt
- ½ teaspoon freshly ground black pepper
- ¼ teaspoon freshly grated nutmeg
- 30 large sea scallops
- 3 tablespoons olive oil, plus more if needed
- 1 large leek, trimmed, cleaned, and thinly sliced
- 1½ cups fish stock or vegetable broth
- ½ cup fresh sweet cider (refrigerated, not from concentrate)
- ¼ cup hard cider
- 2 tablespoons chopped fresh ginger
- 1 tablespoon whole coriander seeds
- 1 tablespoon fresh thyme
- Zest of 1 lemon
- 2 tablespoons butter

Apples Make the Meal

moroccan spiced chicken *with* sour cream

YIELD: 4 servings

This is an easy dinner to prepare for family or for company. Serve with rice, couscous, or egg noodles. Reheat leftover chicken gently in a pan on top of the stove.

INGREDIENTS

- 2 tablespoons olive oil
- 1 large red onion, chopped
- 2 stalks celery, chopped
- 6 large garlic cloves, minced
- 1 (4-pound) chicken, cut into serving pieces, skin removed, giblets and liver discarded or frozen for another use
- 2 teaspoons ground cumin
- ½ teaspoon ground cinnamon
- ½ teaspoon ground ginger
- Sea salt and freshly ground black pepper
- 1 cup white wine or chicken broth
- 1 cup tomato juice
- 2 tablespoons cornstarch
- 1 tablespoon honey
- 2 medium apples (Golden Delicious), peeled, cored, and cut into cubes
- 1 cup sour cream, at room temperature

1 Preheat the oven to 350°F.

2 Heat the oil in a large Dutch oven over medium heat and sauté the onion, celery, and garlic for 5 minutes.

3 Lay the chicken pieces over the sautéed vegetables. Sprinkle with the cumin, cinnamon, ginger, and salt and pepper to taste. Combine the wine and tomato juice and pour over the chicken, reserving about ¼ cup.

4 In a small bowl, make a paste with the cornstarch and the reserved wine mixture.

5 Bring the pot to a boil over high heat, then reduce the heat to low and stir in the cornstarch paste and the honey. Cover the pot and cook in the oven for 45 minutes, or until the chicken is nearly tender.

6 Remove the pot from the oven and stir in the apples and sour cream. Return to the oven and cook for 15 to 20 minutes longer, until the chicken is cooked through. Serve at once.

CHICKEN & APPLE GYROS

YIELD: 4 servings

This is a great way to finish off leftover roasted or grilled chicken. (I usually grill two extra pieces so that I do have leftovers.) If you are feeling lazy or tired, don't bother to cook the onion and bell pepper. Leave them raw and serve with the cold chicken as a salad in a pocket of bread or wrapped in a flour tortilla.

1 In a medium bowl, toss the apple slices with the lemon juice and set aside.

2 Heat the oil in a large skillet over medium-high heat. Add the onion, bell pepper, and jalapeños, and sauté until the vegetables are lightly cooked, about 5 minutes. Stir in the chicken and salt and pepper to taste and cook for 5 minutes, or until the chicken is thoroughly heated.

3 To make the tzatziki, stir together the yogurt, garlic, cucumber, and dill in a small bowl. Season with salt and pepper to taste. Refrigerate until ready to serve.

4 Stack the pita breads or tortillas, wrap in a damp paper towel, and heat in the microwave for 1 minute. Alternatively, wrap the stack in aluminum foil and heat in a skillet over low heat for 2 minutes, turning at 1 minute. Slice pitas in half.

5 Spoon the chicken mixture equally into halved pita bread pockets or down the center of the flour tortillas. Top with the reserved apple pieces and spoonfuls of tzatziki. If using tortillas, fold up one side for the bottom end and then roll them up burrito-style. Serve with Sriracha, if desired.

INGREDIENTS

- 2 medium sweet-tart apples (Jonathan, Jonagold, Stayman, Fuji), peeled, cored, and thinly sliced or diced

  Juice of ½ lemon

- 1 tablespoon olive oil

- 1 medium sweet onion, thinly sliced

- 1 bell pepper, seeds and ribs removed, thinly sliced

- 1–2 jalapeño peppers, cut in half lengthwise, seeded, and thinly sliced crosswise

- 2 cooked chicken thighs or chicken breasts, thinly sliced (about 2 cups)

  Sea salt and freshly ground black pepper

- 4 pita breads or flour tortillas, heated

  Sriracha for serving (optional)

TZATZIKI

- 1 cup low-fat Greek yogurt

- 2 garlic cloves, finely minced

- 1 medium cucumber, peeled, seeded, and cut into tiny dice

- 2 sprigs fresh dill or fennel fronds, finely snipped

  Sea salt and freshly ground black pepper

ROAST CHICKEN with APPLES, TURNIPS & GARLIC

YIELD: 4–6 servings

This recipe is from Jim Law of Linden Vineyards in Linden, Virginia. He produces award-winning wines and occasionally hosts "wine dinners" during the fall. This dish, he says, is a proven favorite. He recommends using aromatic Ashmead's Kernel apples, which he grows along with other antique apple varieties in his home orchard. Don't hesitate to substitute Jonathan, Jonagold, Braeburn, or other crunchy, flavorful varieties for this hard-to-find antique.

1   Preheat the oven to 350°F.

2   In a small bowl, combine the paprika, pepper, and salt, and rub the mixture over the chicken inside and out.

3   Lightly oil or spray a roasting pan, add the chicken, breast side up, and arrange the apples, turnips, and garlic around the sides. Trickle the lemon juice over the apples and turnips.

4   Roast until the chicken is golden brown, about 1 hour and 15 minutes. Baste with the pan juices two or three times during the roasting.

5   Remove the cooked chicken to a serving platter. Transfer the apples, turnips, and garlic to a food processor. Skim the fat from the pan and pour the remaining juice over the vegetables. Process to a purée consistency and serve separately with the chicken.

INGREDIENTS

- 1 tablespoon paprika
- ½ teaspoon freshly ground black pepper
- ½ teaspoon salt
- 1 (4-pound) chicken
- 3 medium apples (Ashmead's Kernel, Jonathan, Jonagold), cored, peeled if desired, and cut into eighths
- 3 small turnips, peeled, cut into quarters, and thinly sliced
- 6 garlic cloves, or more to taste
- Juice of ½ lemon

Distillery Lane Ciderworks

Owners: Rob Miller and Patty Power

When Rob Miller and his wife, Patty Power, bought their historic 95-acre farm in Jefferson, Maryland, they were intrigued by the history of the beer breweries and whiskey distilleries that had operated in the region before Prohibition and began thinking about ways to run a distillery again. Instead of planting hops, corn, or barley, they decided to plant apple trees and become the first licensed cider distillery in Maryland. In 2001, they planted 3,000 trees representing 45 varieties, including European heirloom cider apples and American hardy antiques as well as modern-day hybrids developed at the Cornell University Agricultural Experiment Station in New York. While many varieties are grown for their cider and winemaking qualities — Ciderworks has one of the largest plantings of specialty cider apples in the United States — others are sweet and delicious for eating fresh or for baking. "My personal favorite for pies is Bramley's Seedling, while Roxbury Russet and Summer Rambo are as sweet and flavorful as any for eating fresh off the tree," says Miller.

By mid-August, weekend visitors can visit Ciderworks to pick early varieties and also watch how apples are pressed into pure apple cider. The estate-crafted hard ciders are fermented and bottled in the farm's converted milking parlor dating from the 1800s. All of the dry or semisweet ciders, including the champagne-style "Celebration," made from a blend of Russets and Tremlett's Bitter, have an ABV of between 7 and 8 percent. "We don't go in for sweet hard ciders but favor those with a crisp, refreshingly tart finish reflecting the bitter-sharp and bittersweet flavors of the apples we are using," shares Miller. Some of those included in the hard-cider blendings are Sweet Coppin, Bulmer's Norman, and Kingston Black. "I typically substitute a dry cider in any recipe that calls for a white wine. I also use it when brining the holiday turkey," says Patty Power. "And of course, whether baking a pie or garnishing a salad, it's all about the apples."

Hard-cider and homebrew aficionados can also take Ciderworks classes on the first Saturday of each month in spring and summer. Armed with a thirst for knowledge and cider, they spend more than three hours learning about converting fruit into alcohol, pH balances, various yeasts, and the resulting contrasts of flavors. They also go home with enough cider to make a case of bottled hard cider.

Note: Recipes from Ciderworks are on pages 56, 112, 118, and 190.

TURKEY SCALOPPINI with APPLE CIDER & MUSHROOMS

YIELD: 4–6 servings

This is a recipe from Tim Rose, cider maker at Distillery Lane Ciderworks (DLC). Tim grew up enjoying his mother's veal scaloppini. His variation uses almost any thinly sliced meat, hard cider instead of white wine, and some thinly sliced apple to add a touch of sweetness. He also suggests using sliced extra-firm tofu to make it vegetarian-friendly.

1 In a shallow dish, season the flour with salt and pepper. Dredge the cutlets in the flour until heavily coated.

2 Heat the oil in a large deep skillet with a lid over high heat. Sear the meat briefly on both sides until browned. Remove and set aside on paper towels. (If necessary, sear half the meat at a time so as not to crowd the skillet and steam the cutlets.)

3 Reduce the heat to medium-low. Spread a layer of sliced onions in the skillet and top with a layer of the seared meat, followed by a layer of mushroom slices. Lay a sprig or two of each herb over the mushrooms, and finish the layering with the apple slices. Repeat the layers with the remaining onion, meat, mushrooms, herbs, and apple. Pour the cider over the top. If desired, season with more salt and pepper.

4 Cover and cook over medium-low heat until the meat is tender, about 20 minutes. The cider will reduce and thicken with the flour from the meat.

5 Serve hot over egg noodles.

INGREDIENTS

- ½ cup all-purpose flour
- Salt and freshly ground black pepper
- 1½ pounds precut thin turkey cutlets (your supermarket will have these and also precut chicken cutlets if you prefer)
- 2 tablespoons olive oil
- 1 large sweet onion, thinly sliced
- 2 cups sliced mushrooms, preferably portobello
- 2–4 sprigs each fresh rosemary, oregano, and thyme
- 1 large sweet apple (Fortune, Russet, Winesap), peeled, cored, and thinly sliced
- 1¼ cups hard cider, preferably DLC American Extra-Dry
- Cooked egg noodles for serving

Apples Make the Meal

This is an easy and good way to cook pork chops — the lean flesh gains moisture by absorbing the liquids. You can serve the sauce as it comes out of the skillet, or you may wish to purée the apple slices to make a smoother cream sauce. This is a good dish to serve with rice.

PORK CHOPS
with APPLE
cream sauce

YIELD: 4 servings

INGREDIENTS

- 1 tablespoon olive oil
- 4 center-cut loin pork chops, cut 1 inch thick and patted dry
- 3 large garlic cloves, minced
  Sea salt and freshly ground black pepper
- 1 tablespoon butter or olive oil
- 3 medium apples (Golden Delicious, Empire, Gala, Braeburn), peeled, cored, and cut into ½-inch slices
- 1 tablespoon firmly packed brown sugar
- ½ teaspoon ground cinnamon
- ¼ teaspoon ground ginger
- ⅛ teaspoon ground cloves
- ½ cup light cream, or sour cream thinned with a little milk
- ¼ cup apple juice or cider

1 In a large skillet, heat the olive oil over medium-high heat. Add the pork chops and garlic, sprinkle with salt and pepper to taste, and brown for 2 minutes on each side. Remove to a plate.

2 Add the butter to the skillet and melt over medium heat. Add the apple slices, sprinkle with the brown sugar, cinnamon, ginger, and cloves, and sauté for about 5 minutes, or until softened and golden.

3 Add the cream and apple juice, and when, after 3 to 5 minutes, the mixture begins to bubble, return the pork chops to the pan. Reduce the heat to low, cover, and cook for 10 to 15 minutes, or until the chops are tender when pierced with a fork. You can use an instant-read thermometer to check that the pork has reached 140 to 145°F. They will continue to cook from the heat of the sauce. Do not overcook.

4 Remove the chops to a serving dish and pour the sauce over the top.

Apples Make the Meal

PORK TENDERLOIN WITH APPLE-SHALLOT SAUCE

YIELD: 8 servings

If you don't have shallots, use a red onion cut into thick slices. A 1¼- to 1½-pound pork tenderloin will serve four people, especially if you are serving it with a grain or potato dish. I usually roast two tenderloins at a time so that I have leftovers to make into sandwiches, add to a salad, or use in a quick stir-fry or in savory pancakes. And roasting two pork tenderloins is an easy way to create a special dinner for friends.

1 Preheat the oven to 425°F.

2 In a large oven-proof skillet or roasting pan, heat the oil over medium heat. Add the garlic, rosemary, thyme, and salt and pepper to taste. Sauté for 1 minute, just until fragrant.

3 Increase the heat to medium-high, add the pork tenderloins, and sear until lightly browned, about 3 minutes on each side.

4 Scatter the shallots around the tenderloins and cook for 5 minutes.

5 Pour in the apple juice. When it begins to sizzle, pour ½ cup of the chicken broth over the pork. Transfer the skillet to the oven and roast for about 20 minutes, or until a thermometer inserted into the thickest part of a tenderloin reads 140 to 145°F.

6 Transfer the pork to a cutting board, tent with aluminum foil, and allow to rest for 10 minutes.

7 While the pork is resting, heat the liquid in the pan over medium heat. Add the applesauce and the remaining ½ cup broth and stir to loosen any solids left from the roasting. When hot and sizzling, stir in the half-and-half and cook until the sauce is thickened to your liking.

8 Slice the tenderloins on the diagonal into ½-inch-thick pieces. Drizzle the sauce over the meat and serve.

INGREDIENTS

- 2 tablespoons olive oil
- 6 garlic cloves, minced
- 2 tablespoons fresh rosemary (from 2–3 sprigs)
- 2 tablespoons fresh thyme (from 6–8 sprigs)
- Sea salt and freshly ground black pepper (about ½ teaspoon each)
- 2 pork tenderloins (about 1½ pounds each)
- 6 shallots, peeled and quartered
- ½ cup apple juice
- 1 cup chicken or vegetable broth
- ½ cup Unsweetened Applesauce (page 80)
- 1 cup half-and-half

Apples Make the Meal

With this dish, the vegetables are already in the pot, so all you'll need to add when serving is steamed or microwaved potatoes and crusty French bread. Skinless turkey kielbasa is lower in fat and holds its shape very well.

POLISH SAUSAGE, APPLES & RED CABBAGE

YIELD: 4–6 servings

INGREDIENTS

- 2 tablespoons olive oil
- 2 medium red onions, sliced
- 2 garlic cloves, minced
- 1 medium red cabbage, cored and shredded
- 4 medium apples (Granny Smith, Fuji, Jonagold, Braeburn), peeled, cored, and sliced
- 2½ pounds kielbasa (Polish sausage) or low-fat turkey kielbasa
- 1 bay leaf
- 1 teaspoon dried thyme or 1 tablespoon fresh
- ½ teaspoon ground allspice
- ½ teaspoon dried oregano
- ½ teaspoon freshly ground black pepper
- Sea salt
- ½ cup beef, chicken, or vegetable broth
- 1 tablespoon red wine or cider vinegar
- Prepared horseradish mustard for serving

1 Heat the oil in a Dutch oven or a large deep skillet over medium heat and sauté the onions and garlic for 5 minutes.

2 Stir in the cabbage and sauté for 5 minutes.

3 Stir in the apples. Place the kielbasa over the cabbage mixture and add the bay leaf, thyme, allspice, oregano, pepper, and salt to taste. Pour in the broth and vinegar, cover the pot, and bring to a boil over high heat. Reduce the heat to low and simmer for 30 to 40 minutes.

4 Meanwhile, warm a serving platter. Remove the kielbasa and cut into serving pieces. Arrange the cabbage mixture on the platter and top with the kielbasa. Serve with horseradish mustard on the side.

PORK TENDERLOIN STUFFED with APPLES

YIELD: 4 servings

This recipe is another favorite of Jim Law's of Linden Vineyards. You can replace the butter with olive oil, but the flavor will not be quite as rich. The stuffing can also be used in split boneless chicken breasts, which you would bake for only 20 to 25 minutes.

1   Split the tenderloin almost in half lengthwise. Place it between two sheets of wax paper and pound it to about ½ inch thick.

2   Melt the butter in a medium skillet over medium heat. Add the apples and onion and sauté until lightly browned and soft, about 5 minutes. Add the bread crumbs, marjoram, and savory, and toss with the apple mixture until moistened through. Remove from the heat.

3   Preheat the oven to 375°F.

4   Season the inside of the tenderloin with the salt and pepper and spread the apple stuffing over the surface.

5   Roll the tenderloin lengthwise and tie with kitchen string. Return the skillet to medium heat. Add the teaspoon of oil and brown the pork on all sides, drizzling in a little more oil if necessary. Place in a baking dish.

6   To make the glaze, combine the honey, brown sugar, vinegar, and mustard in a small bowl.

7   Pour the glaze over the tenderloin and bake for 45 minutes, basting with the glaze 3 or 4 times. Remove from the oven and let rest for 5 to 10 minutes before serving.

INGREDIENTS

- 1 pork tenderloin (about 1½ pounds)
- 2 tablespoons butter or olive oil
- 2 medium apples (Jonagold, Stayman, Winesap, Fuji), peeled if desired, cored, and thinly sliced
- 1 medium white onion, chopped
- 1 cup fresh bread crumbs, made by processing 2 large slices stale bread
- ½ teaspoon dried marjoram
- ½ teaspoon dried savory
- ½ teaspoon salt
- ½ teaspoon freshly ground black pepper
- 1 teaspoon olive oil, plus more if needed

GLAZE

- 4 tablespoons honey
- 2 tablespoons firmly packed brown sugar
- 2 tablespoons cider vinegar
- 1 tablespoon brown mustard

curried ham & apples

YIELD: 3–4 servings

I have found this dish to be a crowd-pleaser, which means I sometimes triple the recipe. It's an easy dish to make when you have guests and return home after a day out. Have your guests peel and dice the apples; it's a nice way for them to contribute to the meal without getting in the way of your preparations. Serve this with jasmine rice, a mixed salad, crusty bread, and a fruity red wine such as an Australian Shiraz or a California Pinot Noir. Cheers!

1 Heat the oil in a large skillet over medium heat. Stir in the flour and curry powder and cook for 1 minute. Pour in the milk and, using a wooden spoon or wire whisk, stir to make a smooth sauce.

2 Add the apples to the curry sauce with the raisins. Reduce the heat to low and cook for 10 minutes.

3 Stir in the ham and cook for 10 minutes, or until heated through.

INGREDIENTS

2 tablespoons olive oil or butter

2 tablespoons all-purpose flour

1 tablespoon mild curry powder

2¼ cups milk

2 medium sweet apples (Golden Delicious, Mutsu/Crispin, Empire, Gala), peeled, cored, and diced

½ cup raisins

1 (about 1-pound) center-cut fully cooked ham, cut into ¾-inch cubes

Apples Make the Meal

Apples by the Numbers

The 2013 U.S. commercial apple crop was 239.362 million bushels, the twenty-fifth largest since the U.S. Department of Agriculture (USDA) began recording statistics on commercial production. The 2014 crop is estimated by the U.S. Apple Association to be 263.804 million bushels. The record commercial apple crop of 277.3 million bushels was produced in 1998.

Although 36 U.S. states grow apples for the commercial industry, the six top apple-producing states are Washington, New York, Michigan, Pennsylvania, California, and Virginia. Washington State, producing almost 60 percent of the U.S. apple crop, is the nation's behemoth leader, with a record 2012 crop of 154.8 million bushels. New York and Michigan are the second and third largest producers and account for approximately 13 and 8 percent, respectively. Pennsylvania and California are also major apple states, but production is on a smaller scale. Virginia comes in sixth, producing the smallest crop of the leading states.

There are approximately 7,500 commercial apple growers in the United States on 350,100 acres (the acreage fell from approximately 467,000 acres in the late 1990s to 350,100 acres in 2008). Many of these growers are small family farmers who operate their own orchards.

Fresh-market varieties represented 84 percent of the apples harvested in the 2012 national crop. All other U.S. production is converted into processed apple products such as juice, jellies, preserves, sauces, pie fillings, and baby food.

Apples are one of the most widely cultivated tree fruits and the third most internationally traded fruit, behind only bananas and grapes.

The average U.S. consumer eats an estimated 16.4 pounds of fresh-market apples and 33.3 pounds of processed apples, for a total of 49.7 pounds of fresh apples and processed apple products.

Exports of U.S. apples have increased over the past decade to an estimated 27 percent of the fresh-market crop — an estimated 40 million bushels. According to the USDA, this is due to liberalization of export markets, increased disposable income in developing countries, and substantial industry export-promotion efforts. Leading markets for U.S. apples include Mexico, Canada, Taiwan, Malaysia, Indonesia, Hong Kong, the United Kingdom, India, the United Arab Emirates, and Saudi Arabia.

The People's Republic of China's apple industry has continued to produce the world's largest crop of apples, harvesting a record 38 million tons in 2012 — half of the world's apple crop. The European Union and the United States are the world's second and third largest apple producers, respectively. Other major apple producers include Turkey, Canada, New Zealand, Iran, and Chile.

The United States, New Zealand, and Japan are the leaders in apple breeding.

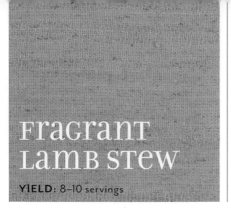

Fragrant Lamb Stew

YIELD: 8–10 servings

This is a good stew to serve with baked potatoes (regular bakers or sweet potatoes). Split the hot potatoes, fork up the flesh, and top with cooked broccoli florets tossed with sour cream and a little Dijon mustard.

1 Heat the oil in a large Dutch oven over medium heat and sauté the carrots, celery, onion, garlic, and ginger for 10 minutes. Sprinkle with the cinnamon, cloves, cayenne, and salt to taste.

2 Add the lamb and pour in the broth and wine. Reduce the heat to low, cover the pot, and cook for 1½ hours.

3 In a small bowl, mix the cornstarch and water to form a paste and stir into the stew to thicken.

4 Add the apples and cook for 30 minutes longer.

INGREDIENTS

- 2 tablespoons olive oil
- 2 carrots, diced
- 2 stalks celery, diced
- 1 large red onion, diced
- 6 garlic cloves, minced
- 1 (1-inch) piece fresh ginger, minced
- ½ teaspoon ground cinnamon
- ¼ teaspoon ground cloves
- ⅛ teaspoon cayenne pepper
- Sea salt
- 4 pounds lean lamb shoulder, cut into 2-inch cubes
- 3 cups chicken or vegetable broth
- 1½ cups red wine or flat beer
- 3 tablespoons cornstarch
- ¼ cup cold water
- 2 large apples (Granny Smith, Braeburn, Fuji), peeled, cored, and cut into cubes

Apples Make the Meal

The kebabs can be broiled, pan-grilled, or cooked on an outdoor grill. You can also omit the skewers completely and cook the lamb mixture as sausage patties. If you are cooking for kids, they will love these savory treats. The best way to test for just-right seasoning is to take a small piece of the mixture and cook it up for a taste and then add more spices as you wish. Add warm pita breads or the Apple, Dried Fruit, and Israeli Couscous Salad on page 74 for a satisfying meal.

GROUND-LAMB KEBABS *with* APPLE-MINT RAITA

YIELD: 6 servings

INGREDIENTS

- 12 (10-inch) wooden skewers
- 1½ pounds ground lamb
- 4 large garlic cloves, minced
- ¼ cup panko or dried bread crumbs
- 1½ teaspoons ground cumin
- 1 teaspoon ground cinnamon
- ¼ teaspoon ground nutmeg or ground allspice
- ⅛ teaspoon cayenne pepper or hot paprika, or more to taste
- ½ cup chopped fresh herbs, such as cilantro, basil, or parsley
- 2 large eggs, beaten

  Sea salt and freshly ground black pepper

APPLE RAITA

- 1 medium apple (Granny Smith, Fuji, Empire), peeled and cored
- 2 teaspoons fresh lemon juice (a good squeeze from ½ lemon)
- 1 cup thick Greek yogurt
- ½ cup chopped fresh mint or cilantro
- 1 tablespoon honey
- 1 teaspoon ground cumin

  Sea salt and freshly ground black pepper

1 Submerge the skewers in water and soak for at least 1 hour.

2 Make the raita. Using the large holes on a box grater, grate the apple into a small bowl and toss with the lemon juice. Stir in the yogurt, mint, honey, cumin, and salt and pepper to taste. Refrigerate until ready to serve.

3 In a large bowl, combine the lamb, garlic, panko, cumin, cinnamon, nutmeg, cayenne, and fresh herbs, and using your hands, knead the mixture. Add the eggs and continue to mix with your hands until the ingredients are well combined. Season to taste with salt and pepper.

4 Preheat the broiler.

5 Divide the mixture into 12 equal sausage shapes. Push the soaked skewers lengthwise up the middle of the kebab sausages. Place the kebabs onto a baking tray and position 6 inches below the heat source. Broil for 10 to 12 minutes, or until done to your liking, turning them over once or twice. Serve with the raita.

BeeF & APPLe DeeP-DISH PIe

YIELD: 6 servings

My mother varied this traditional pork pie by using beef because the meat breaks down better during cooking, making for more tender bites.

Apples Make the Meal

1 In a medium bowl, mix the flour with the thyme, cinnamon, ginger, mace, and salt and pepper to taste. Dredge the beef chunks in the spiced flour and reserve any flour that is left.

2 Heat 2 tablespoons of the oil in a Dutch oven over medium-high heat and sauté half of the beef until browned on all sides. Remove to a plate. Brown the remaining beef in an additional 2 tablespoons oil.

3 Heat the remaining 1 tablespoon oil in the pot and sauté the onions for 5 minutes. Add the remaining spiced flour and cook for 5 minutes.

4 Add the stock and wine, reduce the heat to medium, and cook, scraping up any browned flour sticking to the pot, until steaming.

5 Add the beef, cover the pot, reduce the heat to very low, and simmer for 1 hour.

6 During the last 15 minutes of cooking, preheat the oven to 400°F. Roll out the pastry to fit a deep casserole dish.

7 Spoon the beef with its liquid into the dish, cover with the sliced apples, and top with the pastry. Seal the edges to the rim with the tines of a fork. Cut a small steam vent in the center.

8 Bake for 45 minutes, or until the crust is golden brown.

INGREDIENTS

- ¼ cup all-purpose flour
- 1 teaspoon dried thyme
- ½ teaspoon ground cinnamon
- ½ teaspoon ground ginger
- ½ teaspoon ground mace or mild curry powder
- Sea salt and freshly ground black pepper
- 2 pounds boneless chuck or beef round, cut into 1-inch chunks
- 5 tablespoons olive oil
- 2 large red or white onions, thinly sliced
- 2 cups beef stock
- 1 cup red wine
- Pastry for a single butter piecrust (page 160)
- 2 medium apples (Granny Smith, Baldwin, Fuji), peeled, cored, and thinly sliced

This meat mixture makes delicious meatballs, too. Just shape the meat into 2-inch balls and brown in 1 tablespoon oil in a medium Dutch oven. Drain off the fat, add ½ cup tomato sauce, cover the pan, and bake for 30 minutes.

curried apple meat loaf

YIELD: 6 servings

INGREDIENTS

  2 slices whole-wheat bread, crumbled (about 1 cup)

  1 medium red or white onion

  1 large tart apple (Granny Smith, Jonagold, York), peeled, cored, and finely chopped

  1 pound ground beef

  1 pound ground pork

  ½ cup raisins (optional)

  ½ cup plain yogurt

  2 tablespoons steak sauce

  1 egg

  2 teaspoons curry powder

  1 teaspoon dried thyme or oregano

  Sea salt

GRAVY

  1 tablespoon cornstarch

  1 teaspoon curry powder

  4 tablespoons apple juice

  Splash of milk (optional)

1 Preheat the oven to 350°F.

2 Place the bread in a large mixing bowl. Using the large holes on a box grater, grate the onion into the bowl. Add the apple, beef, pork, raisins, if desired, yogurt, steak sauce, egg, curry powder, thyme, and salt to taste.

3 Mix well. (I use my hands and squish it together.) Turn into a 9- by 5-inch loaf pan, cover with foil, and bake for 1 hour.

4 To make the gravy, pour the pan juices into a medium skillet. In a small bowl, stir together the cornstarch, curry powder, and apple juice until smooth. Add to the pan juices and stir over medium heat until thickened. For thinner gravy, add a little milk.

5 Slice the meat loaf and drizzle with gravy.

LOUISE SALINGER'S APPLE MEAT LOAF

YIELD: 6 servings

I met Louise when I was living in Westchester County, New York. Salinger's Orchard, in Brewster, was just over the border in nearby Putnam County. I visited regularly throughout the autumn to buy apples, cider, and hot doughnuts. She was a great cook and provided big hearty meals for her hardworking family. When Louise's husband, Bob, died, her son Bruce and his wife, Maureen, took over the running of the orchard. Maureen is still head baker for their orchard market and still makes Louise's meat loaf with homemade applesauce. It's Bruce's favorite and also mine. I often make it in a 9- by 5-inch glass loaf pan.

1   Preheat the oven to 350°F.

2   Place the bread in a large mixing bowl. Using the large holes on a box grater, grate the onion into the bowl. Add the beef, pork, ketchup, egg, 1½ teaspoons of the mustard, and salt and pepper to taste.

3   Mix well and shape into a round loaf. Place in a baking pan and bake for 45 minutes.

4   Heat the applesauce, cider, brown sugar, and the remaining 1 teaspoon mustard in a small saucepan over medium heat until the brown sugar is dissolved, about 5 minutes.

5   Pour over the meat loaf and bake for 30 minutes longer.

INGREDIENTS

- 3 small slices fresh bread, crumbled (about 1½ cups)
- 1 medium red or white onion
- 1 pound ground beef
- 1 pound ground pork or turkey
- ¼ cup ketchup
- 1 egg
- 2½ teaspoons Dijon mustard
- Sea salt and freshly ground black pepper
- 1 cup Unsweetened Applesauce (page 80)
- 3 tablespoons apple cider
- 3 tablespoons firmly packed brown sugar

CHAPTER 6

Apple Desserts

Nothing seems to meet with more appreciation than a fresh-baked apple pie. Fresh apples, lightly sugared and fragrant with cinnamon, fill a tender, flaky pastry. Although "easy as pie" doesn't seem as easy today as it did to our grandmothers, pies are so yummy and beautiful that it is worth the effort to master their making. If you are more comfortable with batter, there are lots of scrumptious apple cakes that will fill your kitchen with good baking smells.

Harvest Apple Pie

YIELD: 8 servings

This is my basic apple pie; the only way I vary it is by using different apples (sometimes I use more than one variety) or by rolling out a very large circle of pastry, placing it in a pizza pan, and folding the pastry over the apples to create a very large, half-moon-shaped pie.

1 Preheat the oven to 400°F and grease a 9- or 10-inch pie plate.

2 Roll out half of the pastry and fit it into the pie plate. Brush with the melted jam and refrigerate.

3 Place the apples in a large bowl and toss with the lemon juice.

4 In a small bowl, combine the brown sugar, flour, cinnamon, and nutmeg.

5 Layer half the apple slices in the chilled pie shell and sprinkle with half the brown sugar mixture. Repeat the layers. Scatter the butter pieces over the apples.

6 Roll out the top crust, place over the filling, trim and flute the edges. Cut 3 steam vents in the center. Brush with the milk and sprinkle with the granulated sugar.

7 Bake for 50 to 60 minutes, or until the crust is golden brown. If the edges of the crust start to brown too quickly, cover with strips of aluminum foil or a pie-crust shield. Cool for at least 15 minutes before serving.

INGREDIENTS

Pastry for a double 9- or 10-inch piecrust (pages 157–160)

¼ cup apricot jam or marmalade, melted

5 large apples (Idared, Jonathan, Golden Delicious, or a mix of several varieties), peeled, cored, and cut into ¼-inch slices

2 tablespoons fresh lemon juice

½ cup firmly packed brown sugar

2 tablespoons all-purpose flour

½ teaspoon ground cinnamon

¼ teaspoon freshly grated or ground nutmeg

1 tablespoon butter, cut into small pieces

1½ teaspoons milk

1 teaspoon granulated sugar

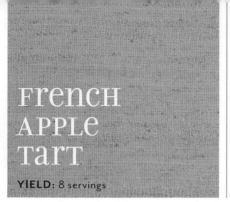

FRENCH APPLE TART

YIELD: 8 servings

This makes a lovely, citrus-accented apple tart that I always vow I'll make more often, because it is so delicious and also so easy to assemble.

1   Grease a 10-inch pie plate or flan tin.

2   Roll out the pastry and fit it into the pie plate. Flute the edges, brush the bottom with the egg white, and refrigerate.

3   Place half the apples in a medium saucepan (don't crowd the apples, or it will take longer for the juice to evaporate). In a medium bowl, combine the remaining apples, lemon juice, and granulated sugar, and toss to coat.

4   To the apple slices in the saucepan, add the brown sugar, orange marmalade, brandy, if desired, and butter. Cover the pan and cook over low heat for 15 minutes. Remove the cover, beat the mixture, and cook for 5 to 10 minutes longer. The mixture should be thick and smooth. Remove from the heat and let cool.

5   Preheat the oven to 400°F. When the applesauce has cooled slightly, spoon it into the chilled pie shell and arrange the tossed apple slices decoratively on top. Bake for 15 minutes. Reduce the oven temperature to 350°F and bake for 30 minutes longer.

6   In a small saucepan, melt the apple jelly over medium heat and brush over the baked apple slices. Allow to cool before serving.

INGREDIENTS

Pastry for a single 10-inch piecrust (pages 157–160)

1   egg white, beaten

10   large apples (Mutsu/Crispin, Winesap, Jonagold, or a mix of 14–15 Golden Delicious and Braeburn), peeled, cored, and cut into ½-inch slices

2   tablespoons fresh lemon juice

2   tablespoons granulated sugar

½   cup firmly packed brown sugar

¼   cup orange, lemon, or apple marmalade

2   tablespoons brandy (optional)

2   tablespoons butter

¼   cup apple jelly or orange marmalade

I often turn to this recipe when I want to serve "apple pie" to family and friends but find I'm short on time. I use a sheet of frozen puff pastry or the little frozen shells. Call these tarts fast food if you want, but they are delicious. I vary the flavor by using black walnuts or pecans and adding grated citrus zest. Serve with vanilla ice cream or frozen yogurt.

APPLE-NUT PUFF TARTS

YIELD: 4 servings

INGREDIENTS

- 1 sheet frozen puff pastry
- 1 (21-ounce) can apple-pie filling
- ½ cup chopped black walnuts, regular walnuts, or pecans, toasted (see note)
- 1 teaspoon grated orange, lime, or lemon zest
- ¼ cup raisins, soaked in apple juice or brandy for 20 minutes (optional)
- 2 tablespoons orange marmalade or apricot preserves

NOTE: To toast a small amount of chopped nuts, place them in a single layer in a medium heavy skillet and cook over low heat for 5 minutes, stirring once after 3 minutes. Remove the toasted nuts to a dish to cool to prevent them from burning in the hot skillet.

1   Preheat the oven to 375°F.

2   Place the pastry on a lightly floured surface and roll into a 12-inch square. Using a sharp knife or pastry or pizza cutter, slice the pastry into four 6-inch squares and place them on a baking sheet.

3   Pinch ½ inch around the edges of each square, bringing the pastry up to form a lip. Prick the crust in several places with the tines of a fork. Place in the freezer for a few minutes to firm up if the pastry seems too soft.

4   Bake the tart cases for 15 minutes, or until they are golden and crisp. Keep an eye on them, and if they seem to be puffing up too much, press the pastry down with the back of a spoon. Remove from the oven and transfer to a serving plate.

5   While the pastry is baking, in a medium bowl, combine the pie filling with the nuts and orange zest; add the raisins, if desired.

6   Melt the marmalade in a small saucepan over low heat.

7   Spread a spoonful of the marmalade in each tart case and spoon the pie filling on top.

Variations

For little tarts, use a package of frozen puff-pastry shells, thawed and baked according to the package directions. Brush with marmalade and fill as directed.

If you want to make your own filling, peel, core, and slice 4 apples and sauté in 2 tablespoons butter over medium heat in a covered skillet for 15 minutes, or until soft.

Apple-Picking Tips

IF YOU ARE INTERESTED IN GETTING THE FRESHEST APPLES YOU CAN BUY, then picking your own (page 99) is the way to go. Here are some tips to get you started:

✳ Call the orchard ahead to check which varieties will be ready for harvesting and whether there are picnic areas and other facilities.

✳ Take your own bags and baskets, unless the orchard specifically states that it provides containers.

✳ Pick apples by giving them a half twist back and forth. This loosens the stem gently without damaging the branch.

✳ When harvesting fallen apples, check for bruises, ants, and wasps.

✳ Wear long-sleeved shirts and long pants to avoid getting stung by wasps and bees that may be feasting on apples pecked open by birds.

✳ Wear comfortable boots or high-top sneakers.

✳ Apply sunblock. Sunny fall days might be mild, but a sunburn is still possible.

✳ Before munching on a just-picked apple, ask the orchardist whether fungal or other sprays have been used recently. If so, wash it before eating.

This scrumptious apple cheesecake in a tart shell is a recipe I received from Ann Kojis Ziff, my longtime friend, who used to bake me the most wonderful birthday cakes when I first came to the United States.

APPLE–cream cheese Tart

YIELD: 10–12 servings

INGREDIENTS

- ½ cup (1 stick) butter
- ¾ cup granulated sugar
- 1 teaspoon fresh lemon juice
- 1 cup sifted all-purpose flour
- 1 pound cream cheese, softened
- ½ cup firmly packed brown sugar
- 1 egg
- 2 teaspoons vanilla extract
- 1 teaspoon ground cinnamon
- 2 large apples (Cortland, Rome Beauty, Jonathan, Fuji), peeled, cored, and cut into ¼-inch slices

1 In a large bowl, cream the butter, ¼ cup of the granulated sugar, and the lemon juice. Stir in the flour until well blended. Press the dough into the bottom and about 1½ inches up the sides of a 9-inch springform pan. Refrigerate.

2 Preheat the oven to 425°F.

3 In a large bowl, beat the cream cheese and brown sugar until fluffy. Add the egg and vanilla and beat until smooth.

4 In another large bowl, combine the remaining ½ cup granulated sugar and the cinnamon. Add the apple slices and toss to coat.

5 Pour the cream cheese filling into the prepared shell and cover with the sugared apple slices. Bake for 15 minutes, then reduce the oven temperature to 350°F and bake for 40 minutes longer.

6 Remove from the oven and cool on a wire rack. Use a knife to loosen the tart before removing the pan sides.

PHYLLO TARTS *with* CARAMELIZED APPLES

YIELD: 12 individual tarts

One packet of phyllo contains two individually packaged rolls of dough. A single roll of phyllo will make 12 tarts, so you need to thaw only one of the individual packages. Allow a few hours for the dough to thaw completely in the refrigerator. Use cooking spray (butter or canola oil) instead of melted butter to moisten the layers quickly and neatly. Children attending my cooking camps have made these tarts with ease.

1   Preheat the oven to 400°F. Grease a 12-cup muffin pan.

2   Combine the sugar, cinnamon, and allspice in a small bowl. Melt the butter in a large skillet over medium heat. Add the apples, stirring to coat with the butter. Sauté for 10 minutes, then sprinkle the sugar mixture over the apples, stirring to combine. Cook for 10 minutes, stirring occasionally. If the apples give off a lot of juice, reduce the heat to low and cook until some of the juice evaporates, adding an extra tablespoon of sugar if necessary to thicken the mixture. Remove from the heat and let cool.

3   For the tart shells, remove the thawed phyllo from the refrigerator. Unroll on a plastic cutting board (the phyllo stays moister on a plastic surface than on wood). Cut through the thickness of all the sheets of dough to make three sections measuring 4 by 10 inches. Cut each long section in half crosswise. You now have six sections, each measuring 4 by 5 inches.

4   Take three or four sheets of dough from each section and pat into the muffin cups. Spray lightly with the nonstick spray. Arrange three or four more sheets across the bottom sheets in the opposite direction and spray again. Arrange three or four more sheets in the opposite direction and spray again. Repeat until all the dough sections have been used. You want at least three layers of four sheets or four layers of three sheets per tart.

5   Fill the phyllo shells with the cooled caramelized apple slices and bake for 15 minutes. Take a peek after 10 minutes, and if the edges of the tarts are browning too quickly, cover loosely with a sheet of aluminum foil or parchment paper and continue to bake until the filling is hot and bubbly.

INGREDIENTS

- ½ cup brown or granulated sugar, plus more if needed
- 1 teaspoon ground cinnamon
- ¼ teaspoon ground allspice or freshly grated or ground nutmeg
- 4 tablespoons butter
- 6 medium apples (Honeycrisp, Cameo, Stayman), peeled, cored, and thinly sliced
- 1 individually packaged roll phyllo dough
- Nonstick cooking spray

Apple Desserts

PUMPKIN-APPLE PIE

If you have a hard time choosing between pumpkin pie and apple pie, you'll want to try this one. It makes a wonderful combination for an autumn dinner. You can easily substitute canned apple slices for the sautéed fresh apples.

1   Preheat the oven to 425°F. Grease a 10-inch pie plate.

2   Roll out the pastry and fit it into the pie plate. Trim and flute the edges. Refrigerate.

3   Place the apples in a medium skillet with the butter, cover, and cook over low heat for 5 minutes. Remove from the heat and drain. If you are using canned apples, simply drain and set aside.

4   In a medium bowl, beat together the pumpkin, cream, brown sugar, eggs, cinnamon, cloves, ginger, and nutmeg until smooth.

5   Arrange the apple slices in the bottom of the chilled pastry shell and pour the pumpkin mixture over them.

6   Bake for 15 minutes, then reduce the oven temperature to 375°F and bake for 35 to 40 minutes longer, or until a knife inserted in the center of the pie comes out clean. Allow to cool before serving.

INGREDIENTS

Pastry for a single 10-inch piecrust (pages 157–160)

2   medium apples (Granny Smith, Braeburn, Newtown Pippin, Northern Spy), peeled, cored, and cut into ¼-inch slices, or 2 cups Canned Apple Slices (page 208)

1   teaspoon butter

2   cups pumpkin purée, canned or fresh

1½ cups light cream or half-and-half

1   cup firmly packed brown sugar

2   eggs

1   teaspoon ground cinnamon

¼   teaspoon ground cloves

¼   teaspoon ground ginger

¼   teaspoon ground nutmeg

Apples and raspberries go well together, perhaps better than any other apple combination. At least I think so until I taste apples and peaches, apples and strawberries, or apples and cranberries!

APPLE-RASPBERRY PIE

YIELD: 8 servings

INGREDIENTS

Pastry for a double piecrust (pages 157–160)

1 tablespoon raspberry jam

1 (12-ounce) package frozen raspberries, thawed and drained, juice reserved

1½ tablespoons cornstarch

¼ cup plus ½ cup sugar

¼ cup all-purpose flour

4 large apples (Rome Beauty), peeled, cored, and cut into ¼-inch slices

English Custard Sauce (page 201) or vanilla ice cream for serving

NOTE: If you use fresh raspberries, you will need 1½ to 2 cups of berries plus ½ cup apple or apple-raspberry juice to use in step 3.

1   Preheat the oven to 425°F. Grease a 9- or 10-inch pie plate.

2   Roll out half of the pastry and fit it into the pie plate. Spread the raspberry jam over the bottom of the pie shell. Refrigerate.

3   Pour the reserved raspberry juice into a small saucepan. Stir in the cornstarch and the ¼ cup of sugar. Bring the cornstarch mixture to a boil over low heat, stirring until the juice is thick and smooth. Remove from the heat, stir in the drained raspberries, and let cool.

4   In a small bowl, combine the flour and the ½ cup of sugar.

5   Alternate layers of apple slices and the flour mixture in the chilled pie shell. Top with the cooled raspberry mixture.

6   Roll out the top crust, place it over the filling, and trim and flute the edges. Cut 3 steam vents in the center. Bake for 15 minutes, then reduce the oven temperature to 350°F and bake for 30 to 40 minutes longer, or until the crust is golden brown. If the edges start to brown too quickly, cover with strips of aluminum foil. Allow the pie to set for at least 30 minutes before serving. Serve warm, with English Custard Sauce or vanilla ice cream.

APPLE-cranberry meringue pie

This is another recipe given to me by my good friend Ann Kojis Ziff when we worked together in New York City. With its pretty pink interior and lightly golden swirled meringue crust, it is a festive holiday pie.

1 Preheat the oven to 425°F. Grease a 9-inch pie plate.

2 Roll out the pastry and fit it into the pie plate. Flute the edges, brush the egg white over the pastry, and refrigerate.

3 In a medium bowl, mix together the brown sugar, flour, cinnamon, and ginger. Add the apple slices and toss to coat. Add the sugared apple slices to the chilled pie shell.

4 In a medium bowl, combine the cranberries and granulated sugar. Using a fork, lightly crush the cranberries. Spread over the apples.

5 Cover the filling with a piece of aluminum foil in which a ½-inch vent has been cut in the middle. Bake for 15 minutes, then reduce the oven temperature to 350°F and bake for 45 minutes longer.

6 To make the meringue topping, place the egg whites and cream of tartar in a medium bowl. Using an electric mixer, beat until foamy. Gradually add the granulated sugar — 2 tablespoons at a time — beating continuously. When the whites are stiff, spread over the hot filling, bringing the meringue to the edges of the crust to form a seal. Return the pie to the oven and bake for 12 to 15 minutes longer at 350°F, or until golden. Allow the pie to set for at least 30 minutes before serving.

INGREDIENTS

Pastry for a single 9-inch piecrust (pages 157–160)

1 egg white, at room temperature, beaten

½ cup firmly packed brown sugar

¼ cup all-purpose flour

½ teaspoon ground cinnamon

½ teaspoon ground ginger

3 medium apples (Idared, Empire, Golden Delicious), peeled, cored, and cut into ¼-inch slices

2 cups fresh cranberries

½ cup granulated sugar

MERINGUE TOPPING

3 egg whites, at room temperature

¼ teaspoon cream of tartar

½ cup granulated sugar

Apple Desserts

APPLE CRUMB PIE

This recipe was given to me by Louise Salinger of Salinger's Orchard in Brewster, New York. Having been married to an orchardist for 40 years and having raised a family, Louise knew more about apples and pies than anyone I'd met. Her daughter-in-law, Maureen, who is head baker for Salinger's Orchard Apple Market, is also an apple-baking expert.

1   Preheat the oven to 450°F. Grease a 10-inch pie plate.

2   Roll out the pastry and fit it into the pie plate. Flute the edges and refrigerate.

3   Arrange the apple slices in the chilled pie shell.

4   In a small bowl, combine the sour cream, granulated sugar, ¼ cup of the flour, the egg, and the vanilla. Beat until smooth and pour over the apple slices.

5   Bake for 10 minutes, then reduce the oven temperature to 350°F and bake for 30 minutes longer.

6   In a small bowl, mix the remaining ½ cup flour, brown sugar, and butter until the mixture is crumbly. Stir in the pecans and sprinkle over the baked pie.

7   Return the pie to the oven and bake for 15 minutes longer, or until the topping is golden brown.

INGREDIENTS

   Pastry for a single 10-inch piecrust (pages 157–160)

5 large apples (Northern Spy, Rhode Island Greening, Fuji), peeled, cored, and cut into ¼-inch slices

1½ cups sour cream

¾ cup granulated sugar

¾ cup all-purpose flour

1 large egg

2 teaspoons vanilla extract

½ cup firmly packed brown sugar

½ cup (1 stick) butter

1 cup chopped pecans

146

Apple Desserts

Top 15 U.S. Apple Varieties

U.S. consumer preference is shifting from the traditional Red Delicious variety to newer varieties such as Fortune, Honeycrisp, Pink Lady, and Jazz, and also some of the latest of the American-bred apples, including SweeTango and Autumn Crisp. According to the U.S. Apple Association in Vienna, Virginia, the following 15 varieties account for more than 90 percent of the annual production. Changes in apple-breeding technology have transformed the appearance and management of today's orchards. The trees are smaller, which makes them easier to harvest, and they bear apples within just a few years, making them a more efficient investment for orchardists.

* Braeburn
* Cortland
* Empire
* Fuji
* Gala
* Ginger Gold
* Golden Delicious
* Granny Smith
* Honeycrisp
* Idared
* Jonagold
* Jonathan
* McIntosh
* Red Delicious
* Rome Beauty

Cortland

McIntosh

Ginger Gold

Empire

Honeycrisp

Gala

APPLE, RHUBARB & STRAWBERRY STREUSEL PIE

YIELD: 8 servings

With a streusel oat crumb bottom crust and the same crumbly mixture used to sandwich a luscious combination of fruits, this is a satisfying pie that is wonderfully easy to throw together.

1 Preheat the oven to 425°F. Grease a 10-inch pie plate.

2 In a medium bowl, combine the oats, brown sugar, and butter until well blended. Take two-thirds of the mixture and press firmly into the bottom and up the sides of the pie plate. Refrigerate.

3 In a large bowl, mix together the granulated sugar, flour, ginger, and nutmeg. Add the apples, rhubarb, and strawberries, and toss to coat. Spread over the chilled streusel base. Sprinkle the remaining one-third streusel mixture over the top.

4 Bake for 15 minutes, then reduce the oven temperature to 375°F and bake for 30 minutes longer, or until golden brown. Let cool before serving.

INGREDIENTS

- 2 cups old-fashioned rolled oats
- ½ cup firmly packed brown sugar
- ½ cup (1 stick) butter, melted
- ¾ cup granulated sugar
- ⅓ cup all-purpose flour
- ½ teaspoon ground ginger
- ¼ teaspoon freshly grated or ground nutmeg
- 2 medium apples (Golden Delicious, Empire), peeled, cored, and cut into ¼-inch slices
- 2 cups sliced rhubarb
- 2 cups hulled strawberries

ALMOND-APPLE STREUSEL

This makes a great potluck dessert. All the layers can be prepared ahead of time and refrigerated, then assembled and baked the day of serving. The almond paste adds a distinctively delicious flavor to this streusel. Many apple varieties work well in this recipe, but I favor those with flesh that bakes into a softer bite.

1 Preheat the oven to 375°F.

2 For the streusel, in a large bowl, stir together the oats, flour, brown sugar, and cinnamon. Add the butter and mash in with a fork or pastry blender until the mixture forms a crumbly mass. Spoon half the mixture into a 9- by 13-inch glass baking dish and press over the bottom but not up the sides.

3 Crumble the almond paste over the top. If the paste won't crumble, slice it very thin.

4 For the apple layer, in a large bowl, combine the sugar, flour, and cinnamon. Add the apple slices and toss to coat. Spoon over the streusel crust and set the dish aside.

5 For the cream cheese layer, in the same bowl used for the apple slices, beat together the cream cheese, sugar, and flour. When creamy, beat in the eggs and half-and-half. Pour over the apple mixture and, using a rubber spatula, spread lightly and evenly over the top.

6 Sprinkle the remaining half of the streusel over the top and bake for 45 to 50 minutes, or until golden. Serve warm or at room temperature with a drizzle of White Chocolate–Vanilla Sauce (see facing page).

INGREDIENTS

STREUSEL CRUST AND TOPPING

- 1¼ cups oats, quick or regular, and gluten free, if desired
- 1½ cups all-purpose or gluten-free flour
- ½ cup firmly packed brown sugar (increase to 1 cup if not using almond paste)
- 1 teaspoon ground cinnamon, or more to taste
- 1 cup (2 sticks) butter, cut into small pieces and softened
- 1 (7-ounce) tube almond paste

APPLE LAYER

- ½ cup granulated sugar
- 2 tablespoons all-purpose flour
- 1 teaspoon ground cinnamon
- 6 large apples (Gala, McIntosh, Golden Delicious), peeled, cored, and very thinly sliced

CREAM CHEESE LAYER

- 12 ounces cream cheese or mascarpone, softened
- ½ cup granulated sugar
- 1 tablespoon all-purpose flour
- 2 eggs
- ¼ cup half-and-half

WHITE CHOCOLATE–VANILLA SAUCE

YIELD: about ½ cup

INGREDIENTS

- 3 (3-ounce) white-chocolate bars (Ghirardelli and Lindt are good choices)
- ¼ cup half-and-half, plus more if needed
- 1 tablespoon vanilla extract

Break up the white chocolate into chunks and place in a microwave-safe 2 cup glass measuring cup. Add the half-and-half and the vanilla. Microwave on high for 45 seconds. Remove and stir until smooth. Add another ¼ cup half-and-half if you prefer a thinner sauce.

cheese & apple tartlets

YIELD: 12 tartlets

The homemade apple purée in this recipe is like a thick, smooth sauce. You could also start with store-bought applesauce and cook it down to a thicker consistency. Or you could use thick apple butter.

1   Preheat the oven to 350°F. Grease 12 small muffin cups or a tartlet pan.

2   Roll out the pastry to a rectangle ⅛ inch thick. Using a 3-inch round pastry cutter, cut out 12 circles and fit into the muffin cups. Pat the pastry up the sides and around the rims of the cups and press down around the pastry edges with the tines of a fork.

3   Prick the base of each pastry cup with a fork and fill each with crumpled aluminum foil or dried beans. Bake for 15 minutes. Remove the foil or beans and bake for 5 minutes longer. Remove and cool on a wire rack.

4   Add the apple slices, sugar, cinnamon, nutmeg, and apple juice to a large saucepan, cover, and cook over medium-low heat until soft, approximately 20 minutes. Remove the lid and cook for 10 minutes longer, or until the moisture has evaporated and the mixture makes a thick purée when crushed with a potato masher. Crush all the apples. Remove from the heat and let cool.

5   Preheat the broiler. Fill the tartlet crusts with the cooled apple purée. Top with the cheddar and broil 4 to 5 inches from the heat for 1 minute, or until the cheese has melted. Serve warm or at room temperature.

INGREDIENTS

Pastry for a single piecrust (pages 157–160)

4   large apples (Granny Smith, Empire, Golden Delicious), peeled, cored, and sliced

¼   cup sugar

½   teaspoon ground cinnamon

½   teaspoon freshly grated or ground nutmeg

1   tablespoon apple juice

3   ounces cheddar cheese, grated (¾ cup)

I love the rustic look of this pie, and I like how fast it is to make. And it's faster still if I opt to use frozen puff or phyllo pastry. The flavorings are very basic; if you like, you can add ½ teaspoon each of ground nutmeg and ground ginger. Or replace the allspice with 1 teaspoon ground cinnamon, or add grated orange or lemon zest.

APPLE ENVELOPE

YIELD: 2–4 servings

INGREDIENTS

- 3 medium apples (McIntosh, Golden Delicious, Empire, Gala), peeled, cored, and cut into ¼-inch slices
- ¼ cup raisins
- ¼ cup honey
- 1 teaspoon ground allspice
- Pastry for a single 9-inch piecrust (pages 157–160)
- Milk for brushing
- Sugar for sprinkling
- English Custard Sauce (page 201) or heavy cream for serving

1 Preheat the oven to 400°F. Grease a baking sheet.

2 In a medium bowl, combine the apple slices, raisins, honey, and allspice.

3 Roll out the pastry to a circle approximately 10 inches in diameter. Spoon the apple mixture over the lower half of the dough, leaving a 1-inch border. Brush the lower border with milk, fold the top half of the dough over the apples, and press to seal. Crimp the edges with the tines of a fork.

4 Place on the prepared baking sheet, brush with milk, and sprinkle with sugar.

5 Bake for 45 minutes. Serve warm with English Custard Sauce or heavy cream.

APPLE PIZZA

YIELD: 8 servings

This is really a single-crust tart, but using mozzarella as a cheese base makes it more like a pizza — a special sweet pizza.

1   Preheat the oven to 400°F. Grease a 12-inch pizza pan.

2   Roll the pastry into a 13-inch circle and place in the prepared pan. Form a rim around the edges. Bake for 10 minutes.

3   Arrange the apple slices on the pizza crust and sprinkle with the cheese.

4   In a small bowl, mix together the brown sugar, walnuts, cinnamon, and nutmeg. Sprinkle over the cheese. Dot with the butter. Bake for 20 minutes, or until the apples are tender. Serve hot.

INGREDIENTS

Pastry for a single piecrust (pages 157–160)

5   large apples (Winesap, Rome Beauty, Fuji, Jonagold), peeled, cored, and cut into ¼-inch slices

½   cup grated mozzarella, cheddar, or Swiss cheese

½   cup firmly packed brown sugar

½   cup chopped walnuts

½   teaspoon ground cinnamon

½   teaspoon freshly grated or ground nutmeg

2   tablespoons butter, cut into small pieces

APPLES IN LOW-FAT BAKING

APPLE JUICE ADDS A NATURAL SWEETNESS AND MOISTNESS and can help you reduce fat in your baking. Your cakes will still be moist but much lower in fat. When beginning to experiment with eliminating some or most of the oil in baked goods, start by substituting applesauce (other fruit purées work the same way) for one-quarter the amount of fat and then work up to one-half the fat called for in a recipe. I substitute applesauce for 100 percent of the fat when making my healthiest breakfast breads and muffins. I prefer the enhanced flavor and the moister texture.

The simplest way to make turnovers is to use frozen puff pastry or a package of pastry crusts. However, homemade pastry is easy to accomplish and is superior to most commercial pastry dough.

APPLe Turnovers

YIELD: 8 turnovers

INGREDIENTS

- 4 medium apples (McIntosh, Golden Delicious, Gala, Ginger Gold), peeled, cored, and cut into ¼-inch slices
- 1 tablespoon fresh lemon juice
- 2 tablespoons butter, cut into small pieces
- ⅓ cup sugar
- 1 tablespoon cornstarch

  Pastry for a double piecrust (pages 157–160)

  Milk for brushing

1 Grease a large baking sheet.

2 Place the apple slices in a medium bowl and sprinkle with the lemon juice. Scatter the butter pieces over the apples.

3 In a small bowl, mix together the sugar and cornstarch. Stir into the apple mixture.

4 Divide the pastry into 8 equal parts and roll out into 6- or 7-inch squares. Spoon the filling onto the center of each square. Brush the edges with milk and fold over to make a triangle. Press the edges together to seal and crimp with the tines of a fork. Using a sharp knife, make a steam vent in the middle of each. Place on the prepared baking sheet and refrigerate for 15 minutes.

5 Meanwhile, preheat the oven to 425°F.

6 Brush the turnovers with milk and bake for 30 minutes, or until golden brown. Serve warm or at room temperature.

LOUISE SALINGER'S APPLE PASTRY SQUARES

YIELD: 20 servings

Louise was always busy baking something. You'll find more of her recipes elsewhere in this book. (See pages 39, 130, and 146.)

1   In a medium bowl, cut the butter into the flour with two knives or a pastry blender, or use a food processor.

2   In a small bowl, beat the milk and egg. Add to the flour mixture and stir to form a stiff dough. Divide into 2 pieces and refrigerate.

3   Preheat the oven to 400°F. Grease and flour a 15½-inch jelly-roll pan.

4   In a medium bowl, mix together the granulated sugar and cinnamon. Add the apple slices and toss to coat.

5   Roll out half of the dough to fit the bottom of the prepared pan and sprinkle with the cereal flakes to within ½ inch of the edges. Spoon the apple mixture over the flakes.

6   Roll out the remaining dough and place over the apples. Pinch the edges together to seal. Brush the pastry with milk. Bake for 1 hour. Remove to a wire rack to cool.

7   While the pastry is still slightly warm, in a small bowl, combine the confectioners' sugar, water, and vanilla. Spread over the pastry. Serve warm or at room temperature.

INGREDIENTS

- ¾ cup (1½ sticks) butter
- 2¾ cups sifted all-purpose flour
- ¼ cup milk
- 1 egg
- ½ cup granulated sugar
- 1 teaspoon ground cinnamon
- 8 medium apples (Granny Smith, Golden Delicious, Honeycrisp, Braeburn), peeled, cored, and thinly sliced
- 1 cup cereal flakes (corn-flakes work well)
- Milk for brushing
- 1 cup confectioners' sugar
- 2 tablespoons water
- 1 teaspoon vanilla extract

Although not as richly flavored as a crust made with all butter, pastry made with vegetable shortening is more tender. This is one of the most basic pastry doughs to make for piecrusts.

INGREDIENTS

3 cups all-purpose flour

1 cup vegetable shortening

3 tablespoons sugar (optional for sweet pastry)

½ cup ice water

Beaten egg white or jam or jelly for brushing

Beaten egg or milk for brushing

Sugar for sprinkling (optional)

NOTE: If the jam is too solid or too cold to spread, melt it first, but let it cool before brushing onto the pastry.

1 Sift the flour into a medium bowl. Cut in the shortening with two knives or a pastry blender, or use a food processor, until the mixture resembles coarse crumbs. Stir in the sugar, if desired.

2 Using a fork, stir in the water, 1 tablespoon at a time, until the dough forms a ball. Too much water or overmixing will make the crust tough.

3 Divide the dough into 2 pieces and flatten into 6-inch disks. Wrap in wax paper and refrigerate for 30 minutes.

4 Roll out one of the disks to a 12-inch circle about ⅛ inch thick. Loosely fold the circle in half, fit into a buttered pie plate (butter browns and crisps the pastry more than shortening), and trim, leaving a 1-inch overhang. Brush the crust with beaten egg white to help prevent the bottom from becoming soggy. Refrigerate until the filling is ready.

5 Roll out the second piece of dough. Carefully lift the pastry and place over the filling. Trim, if necessary. Seal to the bottom crust. Flute the edges, cut two or three steam vents in the center, and brush with the beaten egg. Sprinkle with sugar, if desired. Bake according to the recipe directions.

SHORT PASTRY

YIELD: two 9-inch piecrusts, 6 dumplings, or eight to ten 6-inch turnovers

A really good basic pastry for piecrusts, this is called short pastry because of its high ratio of shortening to flour.

1 Sift the flour into a medium bowl. Cut in the shortening and butter with two knives or a pastry blender, or use a food processor, until the mixture resembles coarse crumbs. Stir in the sugar, if desired.

2 Using a fork, stir in the water, 1 tablespoon at a time, until the dough forms a ball. Too much water or overmixing will make the crust tough.

3 Divide the dough into 2 pieces and flatten into 6-inch disks. Wrap in wax paper and refrigerate for 30 minutes.

4 Roll out one of the disks to a 12-inch circle about ⅛ inch thick. Loosely fold the circle in half, fit into a buttered pie plate (butter browns and crisps the pastry more than shortening), and trim, leaving a 1-inch overhang. Brush the crust with beaten egg white to help prevent the bottom from becoming soggy. Refrigerate until the filling is ready.

5 Roll out the second piece of dough. Carefully lift the pastry and place over the filling. Trim, if necessary. Seal to the bottom crust. Flute the edges, cut two or three steam vents in the center, and brush with beaten egg. Sprinkle with sugar, if desired. Bake according to the recipe directions.

INGREDIENTS

2½ cups all-purpose flour

½ cup vegetable shortening

½ cup (1 stick) butter

2 tablespoons sugar (optional for sweet pastry)

6 tablespoons ice water

Beaten egg white or jam or jelly for brushing

Beaten egg or milk for brushing

Sugar for sprinkling (optional)

NOTE: If the jam is too solid or too cold to spread, melt it first, but let it cool before brushing onto the pastry.

CHEESE PASTRY

Use this pastry for a change when making a plain apple pie, apple turnovers, or dumplings.

INGREDIENTS

- 2½ cups all-purpose flour
- ¾ cup vegetable shortening
- 2 ounces cheddar cheese, grated (½ cup)
- ⅓–½ cup ice water
- Beaten egg white or jam or jelly for brushing
- Beaten egg or milk for brushing
- Sugar for sprinkling (optional)

NOTE: If the jam is too solid or too cold to spread, melt it first, but let it cool before brushing onto the pastry.

1   Sift the flour into a medium bowl and cut in the shortening with two knives or a pastry blender, or use a food processor, until the mixture resembles coarse crumbs. Stir in the cheese with a fork.

2   Using a fork, stir in the water, 1 tablespoon at a time, until the dough forms a ball. Too much water or overmixing will make the crust tough.

3   Divide the dough into 2 pieces and flatten into 6-inch disks. Wrap in wax paper and refrigerate for 30 minutes.

4   Roll out one of the disks to a 12-inch circle about ⅛ inch thick. Loosely fold the circle in half, fit into a buttered pie plate (butter browns and crisps the pastry more than shortening), and trim, leaving a 1-inch overhang. Brush the crust with beaten egg white to help prevent the bottom from becoming soggy. Refrigerate until the filling is ready.

5   Roll out the second piece of dough. Carefully lift the pastry and place over the filling. Trim, if necessary. Seal to the bottom crust. Flute the edges, cut two or three steam vents in the center, and brush with beaten egg. Sprinkle with sugar, if desired. Bake according to the recipe directions.

BUTTER PIECRUST

YIELD: one 12-inch piecrust or twelve small tart shells

This is deliciously like shortbread cookies — rich and buttery.

1 Sift the flour into a medium bowl and cut in the butter with two knives or a pastry blender, or use a food processor. Stir in the sugar, if desired.

2 In a small bowl, mix together the water and lemon juice. Using a fork, stir the liquid into the flour mixture, 1 tablespoon at a time, until the dough forms a ball. Too much water or overmixing will make the crust tough.

3 Flatten the dough into a 6-inch disk. Wrap in wax paper and refrigerate for 30 minutes.

4 Roll out the pastry to a 12-inch circle about ⅛ inch thick. Loosely fold the circle in half, fit into a buttered pie plate (butter browns and crisps the pastry more than shortening), and trim, leaving a 1-inch overhang. Refrigerate until ready to use.

5 To bake an unfilled pie shell, prick the bottom and sides of the pastry with a fork to allow air to escape during baking. Bake in a preheated 450°F oven for 10 minutes (prebaked) or 20 minutes (fully baked).

Variation: Whole-Wheat Crust

Substitute ⅓ cup whole-wheat flour for ½ cup all-purpose flour, and add a *drop* more water, if necessary. You can substitute an equal amount of the less dense white whole-wheat flour, but you may need to add an additional tablespoon of water.

INGREDIENTS

1½ cups all-purpose flour

½ cup (1 stick) butter

1 tablespoon sugar (optional)

¼ cup ice water

1 teaspoon fresh lemon juice

Apple Desserts

I knew Terri Booth when she worked at the U.S. Apple Association. She calls this her "company's coming" cake. It's definitely a fast and winning recipe for a party or when you're expecting weekend guests. Terri's house is like an apple museum, featuring apple memorabilia in the thousands.

TERRI'S QUICK APPLE CAKE

YIELD: 8 servings

INGREDIENTS

- 1 package yellow cake mix
- ½ cup (1 stick) butter, melted
- 2 cups shredded coconut
- 1 tablespoon water
- 1 (20-ounce) can sliced apples, drained
- ½ cup sugar
- ½ teaspoon ground cinnamon
- 1 cup sour cream
- 2 egg yolks

1 Preheat the oven to 350°F. Lightly grease a 10- by 14-inch baking dish.

2 In a large bowl, thoroughly combine the cake mix, butter, coconut, and water.

3 Spoon the mixture into the baking dish. Bake for 10 minutes and remove from the oven.

4 Spread the apple slices over the baked cake crust. In a small bowl, combine the sugar and cinnamon. Reserving 1 tablespoon of the mixture for the topping, sprinkle the sugar and cinnamon over the apple slices.

5 In another small bowl, beat together the sour cream and yolks. Drizzle over the apple slices.

6 Sprinkle the reserved 1 tablespoon sugar and cinnamon mixture over the top. Return to the oven and bake for 20 minutes, or until the top is lightly browned. Serve warm or at room temperature.

Hollabaugh Bros. Orchards
Owners: Hollabaugh Family

Kay and Brad Hollabaugh are part of a four-generation family farming the Hollabaugh Bros. Orchard on 500 acres in Biglerville, Pennsylvania. Their sons and daughters chose to return to the farm to work in their various areas of expertise after graduating from Pennsylvania State University.

The Hollabaughs grow a wide variety of vegetables and fruits, including 120,000 trees planted with apricots, plums, peaches, and apples. Biglerville is in the Adams County apple belt and is one of the top 10 apple-picking destinations in the country.

They also have a farm market bakery where they sell fruit pies, apple dumplings, apple cider doughnuts, and sticky buns. "We bake everything fresh daily," says Kay Hollabaugh, who manages the market as well as many of the office duties.

She is also very active in the Adams County Conservation Association and points out that their farm is certified GAP (Good Agricultural Practices), and as such they follow low-risk advanced integrated pest management in the orchards, allowing them to grow fruits and vegetables with the least impact on the environment. Says Kay, "There is something very special about seeing the first fruits to come from the tree, whether it's apricots or plums, peaches, or apples. The nice thing about working on a farm is that just as things are getting to the point where you are sick of doing them, it's time to do something else. Spring bedding plants arrive and then leave, peaches come and go, apples are here and then gone, and soon it starts all over again with winter pruning and spring planting. I love being a participant in the stewardship of the land."

Note: Kay Hollabaugh's Apple-Nut Cake is on page 163.

Busy with a farm and a young family, Kay also spends a lot of time in the kitchen. This apple-nut cake is her favorite apple dessert because it's rich, sweet, delicious, and loaded with fresh apples!

INGREDIENTS

- 2 cups granulated sugar
- 1 cup vegetable oil
- 3 eggs
- 3 cups all-purpose flour
- 1 teaspoon baking soda
- ½ teaspoon salt
- 6 medium apples (Nittany or Golden Delicious), peeled, cored, and diced
- 1 cup chopped nuts
- 2 teaspoons vanilla extract

TOPPING

- 1 cup firmly packed brown sugar
- ½ cup (1 stick) butter
- ¼ cup milk

1 Preheat the oven to 350°F. Lightly grease a 9- by 13-inch baking dish.

2 Add the granulated sugar, oil, and eggs to a large bowl and beat well.

3 Add the flour, baking soda, salt, apples, nuts, and vanilla, and mix until completely combined. Scrape the batter into the prepared baking dish and bake for 1 hour.

4 To make the topping, in a small saucepan, combine the brown sugar, butter, and milk, and bring to a low boil over medium heat. Stir the mixture together and cook for 2 to 3 minutes, until the sugar has dissolved. Remove from the heat and let cool.

5 Remove the cake from the oven. Immediately poke the tines of a fork down through the cake (about 15 jabs all around the cake) and pour the topping over the hot cake. Serve warm or at room temperature.

CHOCOLATE-APPLESAUCE CAKE

YIELD: 14–16 servings

This is a very moist, rich cake. Take care that the applesauce is not too liquid, or the cake will be more like a pudding. So, if you are using homemade applesauce, make sure it's more apple than liquid. Otherwise, reduce the amount of applesauce by ½ cup.

Apple Desserts

1 Grease a 9-inch springform pan and dust with the graham cracker crumbs.

2 Place the chocolate in a small ovenproof bowl and place in the oven. Set the oven temperature to 350°F and remove the chocolate after 10 minutes to finish melting in the hot bowl. Alternatively, place the chocolate in a microwave-safe bowl and heat in 30-second intervals until melted, stirring each time.

3 In a medium bowl, cream the brown sugar and butter until fluffy. Beat in the eggs, one at a time, then beat in the melted chocolate.

4 Sift the flour, cocoa, baking powder, baking soda, and cinnamon into another medium bowl.

5 Stir approximately ½ cup of the flour mixture and ½ cup of the applesauce into the batter. Continue adding and combining the ingredients until all have been mixed into the batter. Spoon the batter into the prepared pan and bake for 1 hour and 10 minutes, or until a skewer inserted into the center of the cake comes out clean.

6 Cool for 10 minutes in the pan on a wire rack. The cake will shrink. Use a knife to loosen the cake before releasing the spring and lifting the sides from the bottom of the pan. Cool completely before serving.

INGREDIENTS

- ¼ cup graham cracker crumbs
- 8 ounces semisweet chocolate
- 1½ cups firmly packed dark brown sugar
- 1 cup (2 sticks) butter, softened
- 4 eggs
- 1½ cups all-purpose flour
- ¼ cup unsweetened natural cocoa powder
- 2 teaspoons baking powder
- 1 teaspoon baking soda
- ½ teaspoon ground cinnamon
- 1½ cups thick applesauce

This is one of my favorite cakes. Depending on the thickness of the applesauce, this cake can turn out more puddinglike than it should be. If your applesauce is a little on the thin side, reduce the amount of applesauce to ⅔ cup to be sure of the desired texture.

APPLESAUCE GINGERBREAD

YIELD: 12–16 servings

INGREDIENTS

- 1 cup (2 sticks) butter
- 1 cup firmly packed brown sugar
- ½ cup molasses
- 2 eggs
- 1 cup Unsweetened Applesauce (page 80)
- 2 cups all-purpose flour
- 2 teaspoons baking soda
- 2 teaspoons ground ginger
- 1 teaspoon ground cinnamon
- Whipped cream or vanilla ice cream for serving

1 Preheat the oven to 350°F. Grease and flour a 9- by 13-inch baking dish.

2 Melt the butter in a small saucepan over low heat. Pour into a medium bowl. Beat in the brown sugar and molasses. Beat in the eggs, one at a time, then beat in the applesauce. Sift the flour, baking soda, ginger, and cinnamon into the applesauce mixture and stir to completely combine.

3 Spoon the batter into the prepared baking dish and bake for 35 minutes, or until a skewer inserted into the middle of the cake comes out clean.

4 Cool in the pan for 5 minutes, then finish cooling on a wire rack.

5 Serve with whipped cream or vanilla ice cream, if desired.

New York Apple-Bourbon Cake

This recipe has been adapted from the New York State Apple Association. Its spokesperson, Julia Stewart, says this cake gets rave reviews because people love the flavor of the bourbon and spices. If bourbon is not to your liking, you can substitute apple cider or juice.

1 Preheat the oven to 350°F. Lightly grease a 9- by 13-inch baking dish.

2 Place the apples in a large shallow dish and pour the bourbon over the apples. Cover and set aside, stirring occasionally to keep the apples evenly coated with the bourbon.

3 In a medium bowl, beat together the sugar, oil, and eggs with a whisk until completely combined.

4 Sift the flour, baking powder, baking soda, salt, cinnamon, nutmeg, and cloves into a large bowl. Stir in the nuts, the egg mixture, and the bourbon-soaked apples with their liquor.

5 Spoon the batter into the prepared baking dish. Bake for 50 to 55 minutes, or until a toothpick inserted in the center of the cake comes out clean.

6 Serve warm or at room temperature with whipped cream or Breezy Hill Hard Sauce.

INGREDIENTS

- 4 medium apples (Cortland, Empire, Jonagold), peeled, cored, and coarsely chopped (4 cups)
- 1 cup bourbon
- 2 cups sugar
- ½ cup canola or vegetable oil
- 2 eggs
- 2 cups all-purpose flour
- 2 teaspoons baking powder
- ½ teaspoon baking soda
- ½ teaspoon salt
- 2 teaspoons ground cinnamon
- ½ teaspoon freshly grated or ground nutmeg
- ¼ teaspoon ground cloves
- 1 cup coarsely chopped walnuts
- Whipped cream or Breezy Hill Hard Sauce (page 198) for serving

APPLE KUCHEN

YIELD: 12 servings

If you're pressed for time, substitute a cake mix for the flour, sugar, baking powder, and butter. Then add the liquids, apples, and topping.

1 Preheat the oven to 400°F. Grease a 9- by 13-inch baking dish.

2 In a medium bowl, combine the flour, sugar, and baking powder. Cut in the butter with two knives or a pastry blender until the mixture resembles coarse crumbs.

3 In a small bowl, beat together the egg, apple juice, and vanilla. Stir into the crumb mixture. Spread the batter in the prepared baking dish. Arrange the apple slices over the batter. Dot with the pecan halves.

4 For the glaze, melt the butter and honey in a small saucepan over low heat. Pour over the apples and pecans.

5 Bake for 35 minutes. Serve warm.

INGREDIENTS

- 1¼ cups all-purpose flour
- ½ cup sugar
- 1½ teaspoons baking powder
- 4 tablespoons butter
- 1 egg
- ¼ cup apple juice or cider
- 2 teaspoons vanilla extract
- 2 large apples (Fuji, Idared, Cortland, Rome Beauty), peeled, cored, and cut into ½-inch slices
- ½ cup pecan halves

GLAZE

- 4 tablespoons butter
- ¼ cup honey

SIMPLE SPICE FROSTING

FOR A CREAM CHEESE FROSTING WITH A SPECIAL FLAVOR, combine 8 ounces softened cream cheese, 1 stick softened butter, 1 cup confectioners' sugar, 2 tablespoons apple juice, and 1 teaspoon ground cinnamon in a large bowl and beat until fluffy. Spread on top of fruit breads and cakes.

oaTmeaL-APPLe cupcakes

YIELD: 24 cupcakes

As cupcakes go, these little morsels are pretty nutritious — so much so that they can double as breakfast muffins.

INGREDIENTS

- ½ cup (1 stick) butter, softened
- ½ cup firmly packed brown sugar
- ½ cup honey
- 1 cup Unsweetened Applesauce (page 80)
- 2 eggs
- 1 cup sifted all-purpose flour
- ½ cup whole-wheat flour
- 1 cup old-fashioned rolled oats
- 1½ teaspoons baking powder
- 1 teaspoon baking soda
- 1 teaspoon ground allspice

APPLE GLAZE (OPTIONAL)

- 2 teaspoons cornstarch
- ½ cup apple juice or cider
- ½ cup thawed frozen apple juice concentrate
- ½ teaspoon ground cinnamon
- ¼ cup confectioners' sugar (optional)

1 Preheat the oven to 375°F. Line 24 muffin cups with paper liners.

2 In a medium bowl, cream the butter and brown sugar. Beat in the honey, applesauce, and eggs.

3 In another medium bowl, mix together the flours, oats, baking powder, baking soda, and allspice. Stir into the applesauce mixture.

4 Fill the paper cups half full with the batter. Bake for 20 minutes, or until a skewer inserted into the center of a cupcake comes out clean. Remove from the muffin pans and cool on wire racks.

5 If using the apple glaze, mix the cornstarch with a little of the apple juice in a small bowl to make a smooth paste.

6 Add the remaining apple juice to a small saucepan set over low heat. Gradually add the cornstarch paste and cook, stirring constantly, until thick and smooth. Stir in the apple juice concentrate and cinnamon. Remove from the heat. If a sweeter glaze is desired, beat in the confectioners' sugar.

7 Cool slightly and spoon over the cooled cupcakes, if desired.

APPLe STruDeL

YIELD: 2 strudels/10–12 slices

If you like to bake with a firm, tart apple such as Granny Smith, I recommend you precook the slices, because phyllo pastry bakes easily in 30 minutes, not enough time for hard apples to break down. When I attended a course at the Culinary Institute of America in Hyde Park, New York, we roasted diced Granny Smith apples for 30 minutes prior to assembling the strudel. I prefer to eliminate this step and use a less-firm apple sliced very thin. A food processor or mandoline makes short work of this process.

1   Preheat the oven to 400°F. Grease a large baking sheet or line with parchment paper to fit. Place the apple slices in a large bowl and toss with the vanilla. Add the brown sugar, walnuts, raisins, and cinnamon, and stir to combine. Set aside.

2   Use 6 sheets of phyllo per strudel. Keep the remaining 6 sheets of phyllo enclosed in plastic wrap or damp paper towels. Lay the first 1 or 2 sheets of phyllo on a plastic cutting board (this will ease the transference to the baking sheet). Brush with melted butter or lightly coat with cooking spray. Repeat until all 6 sheets are buttered and stacked. (If you pick up two sheets at a time, it does not matter. Just keep working so the sheets don't dry out and crack too much.)

3   Brush the last sheet with half of the melted preserves and sprinkle half of the graham cracker crumbs over the top.

4   Have a long side of the stacked sheets nearest to you to make rolling easy. Spoon half the reserved apple filling down the long side near to you, keeping it 1 inch from that edge and also about 1 inch from the short edges. Fold the left and right edges in over the filling and then roll the filling side over onto the dough and keep rolling toward the top until totally enclosed. It's just like making a burrito.

5   Carefully slide the strudel onto the prepared baking sheet, seam side down, and brush with melted butter or spray with cooking spray. Lightly score the dough into 5 or 6 equal portions. Repeat with the remaining 6 sheets of phyllo and filling.

6   Bake for 35 to 40 minutes, or until golden brown. If the strudels appear to be browning too quickly, lightly cover with a sheet of parchment paper and continue baking.

7   For the icing, in a small bowl, stir together the confectioners' sugar and vanilla and drizzle over the warm strudels. Cut the strudels following the score marks and serve warm.

INGREDIENTS

- 4   large apples (Golden Delicious, Empire, Gala), peeled, cored, and thinly sliced
- 2   teaspoons vanilla or almond extract
- ½   cup firmly packed brown sugar
- ½   cup chopped walnuts
- ½   cup golden raisins
- 1   teaspoon ground cinnamon
- 12   sheets thawed frozen phyllo dough (17 by 12 inches)
- ½   cup (1 stick) butter, melted, or butter-flavored cooking spray
- ½   cup apricot or raspberry preserves or orange marmalade, melted
- ½   cup cinnamon graham cracker crumbs (from about 2 graham crackers)

ICING

- ⅔   cup confectioners' sugar
- 1   tablespoon vanilla extract or fresh lemon juice

APPLE-MOLASSES COOKIES

YIELD: about 40 cookies

Anything that tastes of molasses and ginger takes me right back to childhood. Whereas chocolate cookies and bars were not considered the best fare for school snacks, I was given unlimited freedom to eat gingersnaps. My mother thought they were healthful because they contained molasses, a good source of iron.

1 In a medium bowl, mix together the flour, ginger, baking soda, and nutmeg.

2 In a large bowl, cream the butter and brown sugar. Add the eggs and beat until combined. Beat in the molasses and apple juice. Stir in the flour mixture and beat until smooth. Cover and refrigerate for approximately 1 hour.

3 Preheat the oven to 375°F. Grease two large baking sheets.

4 Using a tablespoon, drop spoonfuls of the dough 2 inches apart onto the baking sheets. Bake for 10 minutes, or until the cookies are lightly browned around the edges. Remove from the pans and cool on wire racks.

INGREDIENTS

- 3 cups sifted all-purpose flour
- 1½ teaspoons ground ginger
- 1 teaspoon baking soda
- ½ teaspoon freshly grated or ground nutmeg
- 1 cup (2 sticks) butter, softened
- 1 cup firmly packed brown sugar
- 2 eggs
- ½ cup molasses
- ¼ cup apple juice or cider

NATIONAL APPLE MONTH

October positively sings of apples and autumn. It's no wonder the apple connoisseurs have turned it into National Apple Month. A visit to the orchards at this time of year is a wonderful assault on the senses. The soft autumn days are redolent with the winey fragrance of ripe fruit and the woody smell of smoke that lingers in the damp air.

APPLe & Date squares

YIELD: 16 squares

You can make these squares with other dried fruits — raisins, cranberries, blueberries, or cherries. Or use a cup of mixed fruits.

INGREDIENTS

- 1 cup firmly packed brown sugar
- ½ cup (1 stick) butter, softened
- 2 eggs
- 1 cup all-purpose flour
- 1 teaspoon ground cinnamon
- ½ teaspoon baking powder
- ½ teaspoon baking soda
- ¼ teaspoon ground cloves
- ¼ teaspoon freshly grated or ground nutmeg
- 1 large apple (Mutsu/Crispin, Fuji, Jonathan, Winesap), peeled, cored, and chopped
- 1 cup chopped dates
- ½ cup chopped walnuts

1 Preheat the oven to 350°F. Grease and flour an 8-inch square baking dish.

2 In a medium bowl, cream the brown sugar and butter until fluffy. Beat in the eggs, one at a time. Sift in the flour, cinnamon, baking powder, baking soda, cloves, and nutmeg. Stir to combine. Stir in the apple chunks, dates, and nuts. Scrape the batter into the prepared baking dish.

3 Bake for 30 minutes, or until a skewer inserted into the center of the cake comes out clean. Cool in the pan on a wire rack. When cool, cut into squares.

APPLE-cinnamon squares

YIELD: 16 squares

The combination of apples and cinnamon is one of the all-time greats. If you like cinnamon, you'll love this recipe — it's bursting with it.

1   Preheat the oven to 350°F. Grease and flour an 8-inch square baking dish.

2   Melt ½ cup of the butter in a medium saucepan over low heat. Remove from the heat and stir in the brown sugar. Beat in the eggs, one at a time, and add the vanilla. Stir in the whole-wheat flour. Sift in the all-purpose flour, 1½ teaspoons of the cinnamon, the baking powder, and the baking soda. Stir to combine. Add the diced apple and raisins and mix well. Pour into the prepared baking dish.

3   In a small bowl, mix together the remaining 2 tablespoons cinnamon and the granulated sugar. Sprinkle over the batter.

4   Melt the remaining 2 tablespoons butter in a small saucepan over low heat and drizzle over the sugar and cinnamon.

5   Bake for 30 minutes, or until a skewer inserted into the center of the cake comes out clean. Cool in the pan on a wire rack. When cool, cut into squares.

INGREDIENTS

- ½ cup (1 stick) plus 2 tablespoons butter
- ¾ cup firmly packed brown sugar
- 2 eggs
- 2 teaspoons vanilla extract
- ⅓ cup whole-wheat flour
- ⅔ cup all-purpose flour
- 2 tablespoons plus 1½ teaspoons ground cinnamon
- 1 teaspoon baking powder
- ½ teaspoon baking soda
- 1 large apple (Rome Beauty, Jonagold, Fuji), peeled, cored, and diced
- ½ cup raisins or dried cranberries
- ½ cup granulated sugar

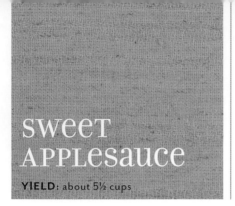

SWEET APPLESAUCE

YIELD: about 5½ cups

A dessert applesauce, this is delicious all on its own.

1 Place the apples in a large saucepan with the honey, apple juice, butter, cinnamon, and ginger. Cover the pot and simmer over low heat for approximately 30 minutes, or until the apples are tender.

2 Purée in a blender or food processor. Stir in more honey to taste, if desired.

INGREDIENTS

10 medium apples (any kind except Red Delicious or summer-harvested apples such as Lodi, Tydeman's Red, Puritan), peeled, cored, and each cut into quarters

⅓ cup honey, plus more if desired, or ½ cup firmly packed brown sugar

3 tablespoons apple juice or cider

3 tablespoons butter, cut into small pieces

½ teaspoon ground cinnamon

½ teaspoon ground ginger

So good and so easy, there's no excuse not to make dessert from scratch — especially if you substitute apple-pie filling for fresh apple slices, because you'll knock almost 10 minutes off the preparation.

MAPLE APPLE CRISP

YIELD: 6–8 servings

INGREDIENTS

- 1 cup of your favorite granola
- ½ cup firmly packed dark brown sugar
- ½ cup old-fashioned rolled oats
- ½ cup chopped walnuts or pecans
- 1 teaspoon ground cinnamon
- ½ cup (1 stick) butter, at room temperature
- 4 large apples (Winesap, Idared, Northern Spy, Braeburn), peeled, cored, and cut into ¼-inch slices
- ⅓ cup maple syrup
- 1 tablespoon fresh lemon juice
- Vanilla ice cream for serving

1 Preheat the oven to 400°F. Grease a deep 2-quart baking dish.

2 In a medium bowl, combine the granola, brown sugar, oats, nuts, and cinnamon. Using your fingers, blend in the butter.

3 Place the apple slices in the prepared baking dish and sprinkle with the maple syrup and lemon juice.

4 Cover the apples with the granola mixture and bake for 40 minutes, or until the apples are tender when pierced with a sharp knife. Serve warm with ice cream, if desired.

APPLE-BLACKBERRY CRISP

There are pounds of blackberries for the picking on the hills behind my family's house in Argyll, Scotland. Although most are used for jams and jellies, some find their way into dessert dishes such as this delectable one.

1 Preheat the oven to 400°F. Grease a deep 2-quart baking dish.

2 Place the apple slices in a medium saucepan, cover, and cook over low heat for 10 minutes. Transfer to the prepared baking dish and add the blackberries.

3 In a small bowl, combine the granulated sugar and the 2 tablespoons flour. Stir into the apple slices and blackberries.

4 In a medium bowl, mix together the 1 cup flour, the brown sugar, and cinnamon. Using two knives or a pastry blender, cut in the butter until the mixture resembles coarse crumbs.

5 Sprinkle over the apple filling and bake for 30 minutes, or until the crumbs are golden brown. Serve warm with English Custard Sauce or heavy cream.

INGREDIENTS

4 large apples (Rome Beauty, Winesap, Idared), peeled, cored, and cut into ¼-inch slices

1½ cups blackberries

½ cup granulated sugar

1 cup plus 2 tablespoons all-purpose flour

½ cup firmly packed brown sugar

1 teaspoon ground cinnamon

½ cup (1 stick) butter

English Custard Sauce (page 201) or heavy cream for serving

APPLe-RHUBarB SLUMP

Slump is a New England name for a fruit dessert topped with a sweet dumpling mixture. On Cape Cod, traditionalists call slumps grunts. *In other parts of the country, they fall under the heading of* cobblers. *No matter what they're called, they all taste good.*

1 Preheat the oven to 400°F. Grease a 2-quart baking dish.

2 Place the apples, rhubarb, the ¾ cup sugar, the cinnamon, ginger, and cloves in a medium saucepan and cook, covered, over low heat for about 10 minutes, stirring once or twice, or until the apple slices are tender but not falling apart.

3 Sift the flour and baking powder into a medium bowl. Stir in the 2 tablespoons sugar. Using two knives or a pastry blender, cut in the butter until the mixture resembles coarse crumbs. Add the milk and vanilla and stir until just blended. Do not overmix.

4 Pour the hot apple-rhubarb mixture into the prepared baking dish and spoon the dough in dollops over the top.

5 Bake for 25 to 30 minutes, or until golden. Serve warm with English Custard Sauce or whipped cream.

INGREDIENTS

- 4 medium apples (McIntosh, Golden Delicious), peeled, cored, and cut into ½-inch slices
- 2 cups chopped (1-inch pieces) rhubarb
- ¾ cup plus 2 tablespoons sugar
- ½ teaspoon ground cinnamon
- ½ teaspoon ground ginger
- ¼ teaspoon ground cloves
- 1 cup all-purpose flour
- 1½ teaspoons baking powder
- 3 tablespoons butter
- ½ cup milk
- 2 teaspoons vanilla extract
- English Custard Sauce (page 201) or heavy cream for serving

Working every day at Haight Orchards in Croton Falls, New York, Barbara didn't have much time for fancy cooking. Her recipe for apple cobbler is simple and superb.

BarBara MULLIN'S APPLe COBBLer

YIELD: 8 servings

INGREDIENTS

- 6 large apples (Jonathan), peeled, cored, and cut into ¼-inch slices
- 1 cup all-purpose flour
- ½ cup firmly packed brown sugar
- ½ cup granulated sugar
- 1 teaspoon baking powder
- 1 teaspoon ground cinnamon
- 1 egg
- 5 tablespoons butter
- Ice cream, vanilla yogurt, custard, or cream for serving

1 Preheat the oven to 350°F. Grease a 2-quart baking dish.

2 Place the apple slices in the prepared baking dish.

3 In a medium bowl, combine the flour, brown sugar, granulated sugar, baking powder, and cinnamon. In a small bowl, beat the egg lightly. Stir into the sugar mixture. Spoon the batter over the sliced apples.

4 Melt the butter in a small saucepan over medium-low heat and drizzle over the batter.

5 Bake for 45 minutes. The apples will be tender and the topping golden. Serve warm or cold with your favorite accompaniment.

JOHNNY APPLESEED

THE MOST FAMOUS APPLE-SEED SOWER WAS JOHN CHAPMAN, or Johnny Appleseed, as everyone came to know him. Born in Massachusetts in 1774, he left home at an early age to follow the pioneers to the new frontiers with the intention of teaching the Bible and planting apple nurseries from seeds and cuttings. He accomplished his mission, and when he died in Indiana in 1854, he was making his customary rounds of his many apple trees.

APPLE-APRICOT COBBLER

YIELD: 8 servings

A cobbler topping is somewhere between cake and biscuit batter, so it develops a slightly crusty texture. This apple-apricot cobbler is one of my favorites, especially with the bright touch of orange juice.

1 Preheat the oven to 375°F. Grease a 2-quart baking dish.

2 Cut the apricots in half, place in a medium saucepan, and cover with the orange juice. Add the apple slices to the apricots along with the ½ cup brown sugar, the allspice, cloves, and ginger. Mix well and simmer over low heat for 10 minutes.

3 In a medium bowl, beat the butter and granulated sugar until fluffy. Beat in the eggs, one at a time, and stir in the vanilla. Stir in the flour and baking powder and beat until blended.

4 Spread the apple mixture in the prepared baking dish and cover with the batter. Sprinkle the top with the 1 tablespoon brown sugar.

5 Bake for 40 minutes, or until the crust is golden brown.

INGREDIENTS

- 1 cup dried apricots
- ½ cup orange juice
- 5 large apples (Jonagold, Fuji, Braeburn, Gala, or a mix of several), peeled, cored, and cut into ¼-inch slices
- ½ cup plus 1 tablespoon firmly packed brown sugar
- ½ teaspoon ground allspice
- ¼ teaspoon ground cloves
- ¼ teaspoon ground ginger
- ¾ cup (1½ sticks) butter, softened
- ¾ cup granulated sugar
- 2 eggs
- 1 tablespoon vanilla extract
- 1½ cups sifted all-purpose flour
- 2 teaspoons baking powder

Apple Desserts

ENGLISH APPLE CRUMBLE

YIELD: 8 servings

I grew up eating my mother's fruit crumble. It's like a crisp but not as rich. She would use all apples or whatever other fruits were growing in the garden — rhubarb, blackberries, raspberries, gooseberries, and sometimes a combination of whatever was in season.

1   Preheat the oven to 400°F. Grease a 2-quart baking dish.

2   Place the apple slices in a medium saucepan with the ⅓ cup sugar, the lemon juice, and the cinnamon. Cook over low heat, stirring once or twice, for 10 minutes, or until the apple slices are tender but not falling apart. Spoon into the prepared baking dish.

3   In a small bowl, combine the flour and the ¼ cup sugar. Cut in the butter with two knives or a pastry blender until the mixture is crumbly. Sprinkle over the apples. (I like to sprinkle the crumbs with 2 teaspoons sugar.)

4   Bake for 30 minutes, or until golden brown.

INGREDIENTS

- 6 medium tart apples (Granny Smith, Rhode Island Greening, Bramley, Twenty Ounce), peeled, cored, and cut into ½-inch slices
- ⅓ cup plus ¼ cup sugar
- Juice of ½ lemon
- 1 teaspoon ground cinnamon
- ¾ cup all-purpose flour
- 4 tablespoons butter
- Sugar for sprinkling (optional)

APPLE-RAISIN CRUNCH

YIELD: 8 servings

For a really decadent crunch, crisp, or cobbler, drizzle a few tablespoons of melted butter over the top before popping it into the oven.

INGREDIENTS

- 4 medium apples (Granny Smith, Newtown Pippin, Northern Spy, Braeburn), peeled, cored, and cut into ¼-inch slices
- 1 cup golden raisins
- ¼ cup orange juice
- 1 cup plus 2 tablespoons firmly packed brown sugar
- 1 teaspoon ground allspice
- 1 teaspoon grated orange zest
- 1 cup all-purpose flour
- ¾ cup old-fashioned rolled oats
- ½ teaspoon ground cinnamon
- ½ cup (1 stick) butter

1 Preheat the oven to 400°F. Grease a 2-quart baking dish.

2 In the prepared baking dish, combine the apple slices with the raisins, orange juice, the 2 tablespoons brown sugar, the allspice, and the orange zest.

3 In a medium bowl, mix together the flour, the 1 cup brown sugar, the oats, and the cinnamon. Cut in the butter with two knives or a pastry blender until the mixture is crumbly. Sprinkle over the apples and raisins.

4 Bake for 30 minutes, or until the top is golden.

APPLES AND LOVE

It's said that the game of bobbing for apples began as a Celtic New Year's tradition for trying to determine one's future spouse.

JOHNNY APPLESEED SQUARES

YIELD: 8 servings

This is another fast and easy recipe from the files of the U.S. Apple Association. It appeals to me because I love sweetened condensed milk, and because it can be thrown together in the blink of an eye. You don't need to peel the apples if they have thin skins.

Apple Desserts

1 Preheat the oven to 325°F. Lightly grease a 9-inch square baking dish.

2 In a medium bowl, combine the apple slices with the condensed milk and cinnamon.

3 Measure 1 cup of the biscuit mix into a medium bowl and cut in ½ cup of the butter with two knives or a pastry blender until it resembles large crumbs. Stir in the apple mixture and spoon the batter into the prepared baking dish.

4 In a small bowl, combine the remaining ½ cup biscuit mix with the brown sugar. Cut in the remaining 2 tablespoons butter until crumbly. Stir in the nuts.

5 Sprinkle the nut mixture over the apple batter and bake for 50 to 60 minutes, or until a skewer inserted into the center of the cake comes out clean.

6 Cut into squares and serve warm with vanilla yogurt or ice cream.

INGREDIENTS

- 5 medium apples (a mix of your favorites), peeled if desired, cored, and sliced (about 6 cups)
- 1 (14-ounce) can sweetened condensed milk
- 1 teaspoon ground cinnamon
- 1½ cups biscuit baking mix
- ½ cup (1 stick) plus 2 tablespoons butter, chilled
- ½ cup firmly packed brown sugar
- ½ cup chopped walnuts or pecans
- Vanilla yogurt or ice cream for serving

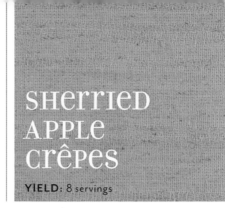

sherried apple crêpes

YIELD: 8 servings

The whipped cream folded into the filling makes these very special party crêpes.

INGREDIENTS

- 4 small apples (McIntosh, Golden Delicious), peeled, cored, and thinly sliced
- ¼ cup apricot jam
- ¼ cup granulated sugar
- 3 tablespoons golden raisins
- 2 tablespoons slivered blanched almonds
- 1 tablespoon apple juice or water
- ½ teaspoon ground cinnamon
- ¼ teaspoon freshly grated or ground nutmeg
- 8 crêpes (page 30)
- 1 cup heavy cream
- 2 tablespoons confectioners' sugar
- 1 tablespoon sherry

1 In a medium saucepan, combine the apple slices with the jam, granulated sugar, raisins, almonds, apple juice, cinnamon, and nutmeg. Cook over low heat, stirring occasionally, for 10 to 15 minutes, or until the apples are soft and the mixture is thick. Let cool.

2 Make the crêpes following the dessert variation of the basic recipe on page 30.

3 In a medium bowl, whip the cream until thickened, stir in the confectioners' sugar and sherry, and continue beating until soft peaks form.

4 Fold half of the whipped cream into the cooled apple mixture. Spread the filling over the crêpes, fold in half, then in half again to form triangles. Top each crêpe with a spoonful of the remaining whipped cream.

MERINGUE-TOPPED BAKED APPLES

YIELD: 8 servings

This dessert has always been a favorite with my daughter, Wendy. Not one for cakes, she loves any meringue dessert. Because I didn't make this recipe regularly, it encouraged her to start baking at a very early age.

1   Preheat the oven to 350°F. Grease a 9- by 13-inch baking dish.

2   Arrange the apple halves, cut side up, in the prepared baking dish.

3   Heat the apple juice, honey, butter, cinnamon, and nutmeg in a small saucepan, stirring over low heat until the butter has melted. Pour over the apples. Cover with aluminum foil and bake for 15 minutes. Remove the foil and bake for 15 minutes longer, or until tender.

4   In a wide bowl, beat the egg whites with the cream of tartar until foamy. Add the sugar, 2 tablespoons at a time, and continue beating until soft peaks form.

5   Spoon the meringue over each warm apple half and bake for 10 minutes, or until the meringue is tinged golden brown. Serve warm.

INGREDIENTS

- 4 medium apples (Jonathan, Idared, Braeburn), cored and cut in half
- ¼ cup apple juice or cider
- ¼ cup honey
- 2 tablespoons butter
- ½ teaspoon ground cinnamon
- ½ teaspoon freshly grated or ground nutmeg
- 3 egg whites, at room temperature
- ¼ teaspoon cream of tartar
- ¼ cup sugar

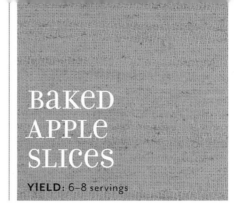

BAKED APPLE SLICES

YIELD: 6–8 servings

When you want a very simple dessert that is neither heavy nor rich, this is a good one to choose. Moreover, you can eat the leftovers for breakfast or serve them as a side dish at dinner.

INGREDIENTS

- 6 large apples (Mutsu/Crispin, Jonagold, Idared, Rome Beauty), cored and each cut into 6 wedges
- ½ cup firmly packed brown sugar or maple sugar
- ¼ cup sifted all-purpose flour
- 1 teaspoon ground cinnamon
- ¼ teaspoon ground cloves
- ¼ teaspoon ground ginger
- 4 tablespoons butter
- ¼ cup apple juice or cider

1 Preheat the oven to 350°F. Grease a large baking dish.

2 Arrange the apple wedges in a single layer in the prepared baking dish.

3 In a small bowl, mix together the brown sugar, flour, cinnamon, cloves, and ginger. Sprinkle over the apples.

4 Melt the butter in a small saucepan over low heat and stir in the apple juice. Drizzle over the apples. Cover the dish with aluminum foil.

5 Bake for 20 minutes. Uncover and bake for 15 minutes longer. Serve warm.

Calvados & Cider Soufflé

YIELD: 6 servings

This recipe is from Patty Power, who, with husband Rob Miller, owns the Distillery Lane Ciderworks in Jefferson, Maryland. Read about them on page 117.

1 Preheat the oven to 425°F. Brush six 6-ounce soufflé cups with the butter and sprinkle with 3 tablespoons of the sugar.

2 Bring the cider to a boil in a small saucepan over medium heat. Continue cooking at a low boil until the cider is reduced to 2 syrupy tablespoons.

3 Combine the milk and the remaining 4 tablespoons sugar in a medium cold saucepan and stir until the sugar is dissolved. Stir in the flour completely, then add the cloves, ginger, nutmeg, and cider reduction. Cook this mixture over medium heat, stirring occasionally, until the sauce thickens. Remove from the heat. Stir in the Calvados and the egg yolks.

4 In a large bowl, whip the egg whites until firm peaks form — do not overbeat. Fold approximately one-quarter of the beaten whites into the mixture in the saucepan, then carefully fold this mixture into the remaining beaten whites — do not overmix. Divide this final mixture among the six soufflé cups. Run a knife around the edge of each cup to help with the rising. Carefully slide 2 or 3 apple slices into the center of each soufflé. Bake for 10 minutes, or until the soufflés have risen and are golden brown on top.

5 For the Calvados whipped cream, in a medium bowl, combine the cream and sugar and whip until soft peaks form. Add the Calvados and whip until incorporated. Serve with the soufflés.

INGREDIENTS

SOUFFLÉ

- 2 tablespoons butter, melted
- 7 tablespoons sugar
- ¾ cup apple cider
- 1¼ cups milk
- 3 tablespoons all-purpose flour
- ⅛ teaspoon ground cloves
- ⅛ teaspoon ground ginger
- ⅛ teaspoon freshly grated or ground nutmeg
- 2 tablespoons Calvados
- 6 egg yolks, lightly beaten
- 12 egg whites
- 1 medium apple (we recommend a tart variety such as Bramley's Seedling), peeled, cored, and thinly sliced

CALVADOS WHIPPED CREAM

- ½ cup heavy cream
- 1 tablespoon confectioners' sugar
- 2 tablespoons Calvados

vanilla soufflé

YIELD: 8 servings

Not your usual soufflé, this uses caramelized apple slices to create a sauce.

Apple Desserts

1 Preheat the oven to 400°F. Grease a 1½-quart soufflé dish. In a small bowl, mix together the ⅓ cup sugar with the cinnamon. Set aside.

2 In a large skillet, melt 4 tablespoons of the butter over medium heat and sauté the apples for 5 minutes. Sprinkle the sugar and cinnamon mixture over the apples and sauté until they begin to caramelize and are tender, about 10 minutes. The mixture will be syrupy. Spoon into the prepared soufflé dish.

3 Bring the milk and the remaining 3 tablespoons butter almost to a boil in a medium saucepan over medium-high heat. Remove from the heat.

4 In a medium bowl, combine the ¼ cup sugar and the flour. Beat egg yolks and vanilla together in a small bowl, and then stir them into the sugar mixture. Pour in the milk mixture and beat for 30 seconds.

5 Pour the mixture into the same saucepan and cook over low heat, stirring constantly, for 2 minutes, or until thickened. Do not overcook, or the eggs will scramble.

6 Using a wire whisk or an electric beater, beat the egg whites in a large bowl with the cream of tartar until they form smooth, shiny peaks. Stir approximately one-third of the beaten whites into the egg yolk mixture, then carefully and quickly fold in the rest.

7 Spoon the soufflé over the apple base and bake for 15 minutes, until puffed and golden. Serve immediately. Sprinkle with the confectioners' sugar, if desired.

INGREDIENTS

- ⅓ cup plus ¼ cup sugar
- 1 teaspoon ground cinnamon
- 7 tablespoons butter
- 4 medium apples (Gala, Braeburn, Empire, Golden Delicious), peeled, cored, and cut into ½-inch slices
- ⅔ cup milk
- 3 tablespoons sifted all-purpose flour
- 5 eggs, at room temperature and separated
- 1 tablespoon vanilla extract
- ¼ teaspoon cream of tartar
- 1 tablespoon confectioners' sugar (optional)

APPLe-cinnamon SOUFFLÉ

YIELD: 4 servings

This is a very easy soufflé to make. For an adult dessert, reduce the milk by 2 tablespoons and add 2 tablespoons applejack or Calvados.

INGREDIENTS

Nonstick cooking spray

¾ cup milk

3 tablespoons butter

¼ cup sugar

3 tablespoons sifted all-purpose flour

2 teaspoons ground cinnamon

5 eggs, at room temperature and separated

1 cup Sweet Applesauce (page 176)

¼ teaspoon cream of tartar

1 Preheat the oven to 375°F. Grease and flour a 1-quart soufflé dish. Cut a piece of aluminum foil long enough to wrap around the outside of the dish and wide enough to extend 3 inches above the dish. Tie the foil collar around the dish and use a paper clip to hold the ends together where they overlap. Spray the inside of the foil collar with nonstick cooking spray.

2 Bring the milk and butter almost to a boil in a small saucepan over medium heat. Remove from the heat.

3 Combine the sugar, flour, and cinnamon in a medium bowl or blender. Add the egg yolks and beat or blend until combined. Pour in the milk mixture and beat or blend for 30 seconds. Pour into the same small saucepan and cook over low heat, stirring continuously, for 2 minutes, or until the mixture thickens.

4 Stir in the applesauce.

5 Using a wire whisk or an electric mixer, beat the egg whites in a large bowl with the cream of tartar until they form smooth, shiny peaks. Stir approximately one-third of the beaten whites into the egg yolk mixture, then carefully and quickly fold in the rest until it is evenly distributed but not deflated.

6 Pour into the prepared soufflé dish and bake for 35 minutes. It will be puffed and golden. Gently remove the foil collar and serve the soufflé or at least show it off immediately; it will start to collapse once out of the oven.

TWO SIMPLE APPLE DESSERTS

The apple sorbet is a lovely, light dessert to serve after a heavy meal. While the classic English fool is not quite as refreshing, it is still a light cloud of whipped cream and fruit. Although traditionally made with gooseberries, other fruits are often used with splendid results.

APPLE SORBET

YIELD: 1 quart

2 cups apple juice or cider

2 cups Unsweetened Applesauce (page 80)

¼ cup honey or more to taste

1 teaspoon ground ginger or ground cinnamon

1 Combine the apple juice, applesauce, honey, and ginger in a medium bowl, blender, or food processor, and blend. Chill in the refrigerator for 1 hour.

2 Pour into an ice cream machine and freeze according to the manufacturer's directions. Or pour into a shallow dish and place in the freezer for about 1 hour, then beat the mixture, cover with aluminum foil, and freeze until firm.

APPLE FOOL

YIELD: 6 servings

1 cup heavy cream

¼ cup confectioners' sugar

2 cups Sweet Applesauce (page 176)

½ teaspoon ground cinnamon

1 Pour the cream into a medium bowl. Add the sugar and beat until stiff.

2 Fold in the applesauce.

3 Spoon into individual dessert dishes and sprinkle with the cinnamon.

This frozen treat is very simple to make in an ice cream maker, but if you don't have one, simply freeze the mixture in a dish, purée in a food processor or blender (to break up the crystals), then refreeze.

If you have applesauce on hand, using it in place of fresh apples will speed up the process.

APPLE-HONEY FROZEN YOGURT

YIELD: 5 cups

INGREDIENTS

- 3 medium sweet apples (Gala, Pink Lady, Honeycrisp), peeled, cored, and diced
- ¼ cup apple juice
- 1 small cinnamon stick
- ¼ cup honey
- ¼ cup confectioners' sugar
- 2 cups vanilla yogurt, drained, or thick Greek yogurt
- 1 cup half-and-half

1 Place the apples in a microwave-safe dish and add the apple juice and cinnamon stick. Cover with plastic wrap and microwave on high for 2 minutes. If the apples are not quite tender, stir and microwave for 45 seconds longer. Allow to cool.

2 Remove the cinnamon stick and transfer the apples with their juice to the bowl of a food processor or blender. Add the honey and confectioners' sugar and process until smooth. Add the yogurt and half-and-half and process until combined. Chill in the refrigerator for 1 hour.

3 Pour into an ice cream machine and freeze according to the manufacturer's directions. Serve soft if you like, or place in the freezer to harden.

Apple Desserts

APPLE SPONGE PUDDING

YIELD: 6–8 servings

In Britain and in many other regions, dessert is referred to as the "sweet" or the "pudding." Ever since I can remember, we called it pudding. This is not surprising, because many of our desserts were, in fact, sponge or suet puddings containing fruits or preserves. Apple sponge is one of the classics.

1 Preheat the oven to 350°F. Grease a 1½- or 2-quart deep baking dish.

2 Place the apple slices in the prepared baking dish. Drizzle the honey over the apples.

3 In a large bowl, cream the butter and granulated sugar until light and fluffy. Beat in the eggs, one at a time, then the lemon juice. Stir in the flour, baking powder, and baking soda. Pour the mixture over the apples and smooth the top.

4 In a small bowl, combine the brown sugar, lemon zest, and cinnamon. Sprinkle over the pudding.

5 Bake for 50 to 60 minutes, or until a skewer inserted into the center of the pudding comes out clean. Serve warm with English Custard Sauce, heavy cream, or whipped cream.

INGREDIENTS

- 3 medium apples (Golden Delicious, Idared, Empire), peeled, cored, and cut into ¼-inch slices
- ⅓ cup honey or maple syrup
- 1 cup (2 sticks) butter, softened
- 1 cup granulated sugar
- 4 eggs
- 3 tablespoons fresh lemon juice
- 2 cups sifted all-purpose flour
- 2 teaspoons baking powder
- ½ teaspoon baking soda
- 2 tablespoons firmly packed brown sugar
- 1 teaspoon grated lemon zest
- ½ teaspoon ground cinnamon
- English Custard Sauce (page 201), heavy cream, or whipped cream for serving

MICROWAVE APPLE BREAD PUDDING

I grew up eating steamed puddings made from cake batter or day-old bread. They were dense but amazingly light and usually flavored with fruit.

YIELD: 4–6 servings

INGREDIENTS

- 2 cups milk
- 2 medium apples (Empire, Golden Delicious, Granny Smith, Braeburn), peeled, cored, and chopped
- 4 large slices bread, cut or torn into 1-inch pieces
- ½ cup chopped walnuts or pecans
- 2 extra-large eggs
- ⅓ cup firmly packed brown sugar
- 1 teaspoon vanilla extract
- ½ teaspoon ground cinnamon

1 Pour the milk into a 4-cup microwave-safe glass dish and add the chopped apples. Microwave on high for 3 to 4 minutes, or until the milk forms small bubbles around the sides but is not boiling.

2 Combine the bread and walnuts in a 1½-quart soufflé dish.

3 In a small bowl, beat together the eggs, brown sugar, vanilla, and cinnamon. Slowly whisk in ½ cup of the milk from the apple mixture. Stirring continuously, slowly pour the egg mixture into the remaining milk and apples.

4 Pour the apple mixture over the bread and nuts. Cover the top of the dish with wax paper.

5 Microwave on high for 2 minutes. Remove the dish and stir the mixture gently. Cover with the wax paper.

6 Microwave on medium for 1½ minutes, remove the dish, and stir the edges into the center. Cover with the wax paper.

7 Microwave on medium for 1½ minutes longer. The pudding will not be fully set in the middle.

8 Remove the wax paper. Let the pudding sit for 20 to 30 minutes. Serve warm or at room temperature.

NOTE: To bake in an ordinary oven, preheat to 400°F. Set the uncovered dish in a large baking pan. Add enough boiling water to come 1 inch up the sides of the dish. Bake for 25 minutes, or until puffy and golden.

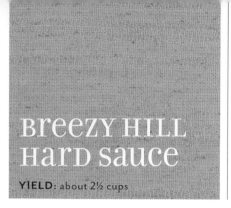

Breezy HILL HarD sauce

YIELD: about 2½ cups

Elizabeth Ryan likes to offer this hard sauce with apple Betty, crisps, and other baked goodies served warm from the oven.

In a medium bowl, cream the sugar, butter, and Calvados until light and fluffy. Chill for 2 hours before serving.

INGREDIENTS

2 cups confectioners' sugar

½ cup (1 stick) butter, softened

2 tablespoons Calvados

Breezy Hill Orchard
Owner: Elizabeth Ryan

For over 25 years, Elizabeth Ryan has owned and operated Breezy Hill Orchard and Cider Mill in Staatsburg, New York. Located in the historic Hudson Valley, the orchard features more than 100 varieties of apples and other fruits grown under her environmental steward-ship. Ryan also operates the 200-year-old Stone Ridge Orchard in Stone Ridge, New York.

Breezy Hill and Stone Ridge orchards are Eco Apple certified by the Northeast orga-nization Red Tomato. The certification means that all of the apples produced from both orchards are certified low spray, as well as indicating the fair trade and fair labor practices of the business.

Ryan, who studied pomology and pest management at Cornell University in Ithaca, New York, has created a showplace for old varieties.

Among her heirloom and antique varieties are Jonathan, Stayman, Golden Russet, King Luscious, and Opalescent. She also grows some of the more modern hybrids, such as Jonagold, Gala, Fuji, Ginger Gold, Macoun, and Honeycrisp. The fruit from both orchards and a line of artisan baked goods and cider are sold at Breezy Hill's farm market, which also features a wide variety of gourmet products and farm produce grown by local farms using sustainable farming practices.

Ryan's sustainable practices include releasing beneficial insects into the orchards instead of using pesticides. She has collaborated with four institutions on several exper-iments related to predator-insect use in her orchards. Besides Cornell University, the University of Vermont, and Rutgers University, she has also worked with the Rodale Institute in Pennsylvania. "To encourage the beneficials to stay, we provide shelter and food for them by allowing vegetation to grow under the apple trees," explains Ryan. "Unsprayed apples are pretty funky looking, but they taste good."

Note: The Breezy Hill Hard Sauce recipe is on page 198.

APPLESAUCE BROWNIES

YIELD: 16 servings

The applesauce adds moistness to these brownies without detracting from the chocolate flavor. If you make your own applesauce, make sure it does not contain too much liquid. It it's very thin, drain it a little or cut back to ¾ cup applesauce.

1 Preheat the oven to 350°F. Grease and flour an 8-inch square baking dish.

2 Melt the butter in a medium saucepan over medium-low heat. Remove from the heat and beat in the brown sugar, applesauce, eggs, and vanilla. Sift in the flour, cocoa, baking powder, and baking soda. Stir to combine. Stir in the pecans.

3 Pour the batter into the prepared baking dish and bake for 25 to 30 minutes, or until a skewer inserted into the center of the brownies comes out clean. Cool in the pan on a wire rack. Cut into squares and serve.

INGREDIENTS

- ½ cup (1 stick) butter
- 1½ cups firmly packed brown sugar
- 1 cup Unsweetened Applesauce (page 80)
- 2 eggs
- 2 teaspoons vanilla extract
- 1¼ cups all-purpose flour
- ¼ cup unsweetened natural cocoa powder
- 1 teaspoon baking powder
- ½ teaspoon baking soda
- ½ cup chopped pecans

Dinner in Britain, whether at my mother's home or at any of her farming siblings' and relatives', was almost always followed by a sweet dish. Pies and baked puddings were accompanied by double (clotted) cream or custard, such as this one. You can also serve this sauce with baked apples and any of the crisps and cobblers. Though it's usually served warm, it can be refrigerated and is simply out of this world when chilled.

ENGLISH CUSTARD SAUCE

YIELD: 2 cups

INGREDIENTS

⅓ cup sugar

2 tablespoons cornstarch

3 egg yolks

2 cups milk or light cream

2 teaspoons vanilla extract

1   In the top of a double boiler, whisk together the sugar, cornstarch, and egg yolks until smooth.

2   Heat the milk in a medium saucepan over medium heat until it comes to a boil. Slowly pour half over the egg mixture, stirring constantly. Stir in the remaining milk, then the vanilla.

3   Place the top of the double boiler over but not touching simmering water and, stirring constantly, cook for 2 minutes, or until the mixture thickens and is smooth.

4   Remove from the heat and pour into a small jug. Serve immediately, or cover the surface with wax paper to prevent a skin from forming and refrigerate until ready to use.

Variation
For a richer custard, in a small bowl, whip ½ cup heavy cream until thick but not stiff and stir into the cooled custard.

Apple Desserts

APRICOT-APPLE DUMPLINGS

Apple dumplings can be made quite easily (especially if you use store-bought pastry), yet most people shy away from making them because they look as though they are difficult to assemble. Not at all. They come together quickly, and they taste like apple pie but make a prettier presentation.

1 Preheat the oven to 400°F.

2 Peel and core the apples, leaving approximately ¼ inch of flesh at the base. Trim the bottoms, if necessary, so that the apples sit level.

3 In a small bowl, beat together the preserves, butter, and brown sugar. Stuff the mixture into the hollowed centers of the apples.

4 Divide the pastry into six pieces and roll out each into a 6-inch square approximately ¼ inch thick. Place an apple in the center of each square of dough and bring the four corners together. Dab with milk and press to seal.

5 Arrange the dumplings, without touching one another, in an ungreased 9- by 13-inch baking dish and pop into the freezer for 3 to 5 minutes to chill the pastry.

6 Brush the pastry with a light wash of milk and bake for 45 to 50 minutes, or until golden brown. Serve warm with English Custard Sauce or vanilla ice cream.

INGREDIENTS

- 6 medium apples (Rome Beauty, Braeburn, Jonathan)
- ¼ cup apricot preserves
- 4 tablespoons butter, softened
- 2 tablespoons firmly packed brown sugar
- Pastry for a double piecrust (pages 157–160)
- Milk for brushing
- English Custard Sauce (page 201) or vanilla ice cream for serving

Apple Desserts

This recipe comes from Julia Stewart, spokesperson for the New York Apple Association. Julia says her guests are always dazzled when she serves this elegant but surprisingly simple dessert.

caramel-APPLE PUFF DUMPLINGS

YIELD: 4 servings

INGREDIENTS

- 1 sheet frozen puff pastry
- 4 medium cooking apples (Golden Delicious or Jonathan)
- 1 tablespoon firmly packed brown sugar
- 1 teaspoon ground cinnamon
- 1 egg
- 1 teaspoon water
- 1 teaspoon granulated sugar

SAUCE

- ½ cup prepared caramel sundae topping
- ⅓ cup toasted chopped pecans (optional; see note on page 137)

1 Thaw and unfold the pastry according to the package directions.

2 Preheat the oven to 400°F. On a lightly floured surface, roll the pastry into a 16-inch square and, using a fluted pastry cutter or a kitchen knife, cut into 4 equal squares.

3 Peel and core the apples. Trim the bottoms, if necessary, so that the apples sit level. Place one apple in the center of each pastry square. In a small bowl, mix together the brown sugar and cinnamon and spoon into the apples.

4 In another small bowl, beat together the egg and water. Moisten the edges of the pastry with a little of the mixture. Bring the pastry up around the apples, pleating or trimming excess pastry as needed, and pinch the edges together to seal. If the pastry feels warm, refrigerate for 15 minutes.

5 Place the dumplings in an ungreased 9- by 13-inch baking dish. Brush them with the egg mixture and sprinkle with the granulated sugar. Bake for 35 to 40 minutes, or until the apples are tender and the pastry is golden brown.

6 For the sauce, in a microwave-safe dish, combine the caramel topping and the chopped pecans, if desired, and microwave, uncovered, on high for 30 seconds, or until heated through.

7 Spoon the sauce onto the center of a serving plate and set the dumplings on top, or drizzle the sauce over the top. Serve warm.

SWEET LITTLE BITES

YIELD: make as many as desired; ½ to 1 apple per person

When you don't have time to bake a dessert, assemble these little bites for a simple sweet ending to dinner or to bring to a party. Feel free to flavor the chocolate with cinnamon, orange zest, or any other flavor you like.

1 Brush or sprinkle the apple sections with lemon juice to preserve the color and add a sweet-tart jolt.

2 Measure the chocolate into a 2-cup microwave-safe glass measuring cup and heat on high for 45 seconds, then stir well. The chocolate will continue to melt and become smooth. If it's not completely melted and smooth, heat again in one or two 10-second bursts, stirring well after each interval. Overheating will dry out the chocolate. Stirring vigorously in the warmed measuring jug is a better option.

3 Immediately dip the apple sections in the chocolate and then into any of the crunchy coatings that appeal to you. Place on wax or parchment paper to set.

INGREDIENTS

Medium sweet apples, peeled if skin is tough, cored, and cut into eighths

Fresh lemon or lime juice; for 4 apples, figure on using 2 limes or lemons

Semisweet, dark, or white chocolate chips or chunks; for 4 apples, figure on using 1 cup of melted chocolate

ANY OF THE FOLLOWING:

Finely chopped nuts (toasted if desired, see note on page 137), such as almonds, macadamias, hazelnuts, pecans, or walnuts

Finely chopped salted nuts, such as peanuts, cashews, or pistachios

Finely chopped crystallized ginger, dried cherries, or dried cranberries

Crushed cocoa nibs, cinnamon graham crackers, cookies, pretzels, cereal, or candy

CHAPTER 7

Preserving the Apple Harvest

IF YOU'VE BEEN HARVESTING APPLES SINCE August, by the time the end of October rolls around, your family may wish it were a forbidden fruit. This is the time to start preserving. From canning apple butter to freezing whole pies, there are a number of preserving options for every apple lover.

Applesauce and apple slices are a cinch to can or freeze. You may decide to make jams, jellies, and butters or, on the savory side, to try your hand at spicy chutneys and relishes.

If apple pies are a staple in your house, unbaked pies can be frozen and later popped, at a moment's notice, from the freezer right into the oven (see directions on page 212). I don't like to freeze baked pies; the bottom crust always ends up soggy.

Canning versus Freezing

Canning and freezing provide long-term storage for apples. Apples will keep for 8 to 12 months in a freezer before they deteriorate in flavor and texture, especially if they are packed in a sugar or honey syrup. Canned apples and applesauce will keep indefinitely, although it is always best to can only as much as you can eat in a year.

Most people find that they don't have freezer space for frozen apple products, so they prefer to can apples. I prefer canning because I like the convenience of having the apples ready to eat or bake with right out of the jar. Frozen applesauce takes quite a long time to thaw.

Canning Basics

Apple slices, applesauce, and apple preserves can be canned in a boiling-water bath, which consists of a large kettle, a rack that fits inside, and a lid. Apple slices are usually processed for 15 minutes in pints, and 20 minutes in quarts. Applesauce is processed for 10 minutes in both pints and quarts. Apple jams and marmalades should also be processed for 10 minutes to ensure a long shelf life.*

Whenever you can fruits or vegetables, you should use proper canning jars, which are equipped with flat metal lids and screw bands. The U.S. Department of Agriculture advises against using bail-top glass lids with a separate rubber seal and metal clamp for canning.

A jar lifter and a wide-necked funnel will make the canning process a lot easier and safer.

After the filled jars have cooled for 12 hours, check each lid for a proper seal by feeling the depression on the lid. If you find a jar that hasn't sealed (check by turning it upside down to see if it leaks), take a clean jar and a new lid, fill with the mixture, and reprocess for the given time or refrigerate that jar and use within a week or so. Reprocessing applesauce will not affect the texture significantly. Don't bother to reprocess apple slices, however; you will end up with mush instead of slices.

With careful use and handling, mason jars can be reused many times, requiring only new lids each time.

*If you are processing food at an elevation above 1,000 feet, you will need to increase the processing time. Consult your local Cooperative Extension office or contact the Cooperative State Research, Education, and Extension Service at 202-274-5000 (www.csrees.usda.gov/extension).

BOILING-WATER BATH CANNING

THE U.S. DEPARTMENT OF AGRICULTURE RECOMMENDS THE FOLLOWING PROCEDURE for boiling-water bath canning for jams, jellies, and similar:

1. **Fill the canner halfway** with water. Preheat water to 180°F.

2. **Load filled jars,** fitted with lids, into the canner rack and use the handles to lower the rack into the water; or fill the canner, one jar at a time, with a jar lifter.

3. **Add more boiling water,** if needed, so the water level is at least 1 inch above jar tops. Turn heat to the highest position until water boils vigorously.

4. **Set a timer** for the recommended processing time. Adjust at altitudes above 1,000 feet.

5. **Cover with the canner lid** and reduce the heat setting to maintain a gentle boil throughout the process schedule. Add more boiling water, if needed, to keep the water level above the jars.

6. **When jars have been boiled** for the recommended time, turn off the heat and remove the canner lid.

7. **Using a jar lifter,** remove the jars and place them on a towel, leaving at least 1 inch of space between the jars during cooling.

canneD apple slices

Canned apple slices are great to use in pies, crêpes, and baked desserts. They are also good in fruit salads. However, peeling apples for canning is a laborious chore. When I am working with large quantities of apples, I prefer to can applesauce. Plan to can about 3 medium apples per quart jar.

1 Wash the jars and lids in warm, soapy water and rinse thoroughly. Prepare the lids according to the manufacturer's instructions.

2 For each quart jar, measure 2 cups water and 1 cup extra-fine granulated sugar into a pan and slowly bring to a boil, stirring to dissolve the sugar. Boil the syrup for 5 minutes and then remove from the heat.

3 Peel, core, and slice the apples approximately ¼ inch thick. Drop immediately into a bowl containing a gallon of cold water mixed with 2 tablespoons lemon juice.

4 When all the apples are sliced, drain and pack into the quart jars to within ½ inch of the top, without crushing the slices.

5 Return the syrup to a rolling boil and pour over the packed slices, again leaving ½ inch of headroom. Run a rubber spatula or a chopstick around the inside of the jars to release air bubbles. Wipe the rims of the jars with a clean, damp cloth and screw on the lids.

6 Process the jars according to the boiling-water bath canning instructions on page 207 (20 minutes for quarts; 25 minutes at 1,001–3,000 feet of altitude; 30 minutes at 3,001–6,000 feet; and 35 minutes above 6,000 feet).

7 Remove the jars and adjust the screw bands to tighten the seals.

8 Leave the jars undisturbed for 12 hours to cool. Test the seals. Store in a cool, dry place.

If this quantity seems daunting and more than you need, opt to put up 10 pounds at a time or share the harvest and do the processing with a friend. Also, using a food mill will be faster than pushing the cooked apples through a sieve.

canned APPLESAUCE

1   One bushel of apples (42 pounds) will give you 16 to 20 quarts of applesauce. Wash and quarter the apples. It is not necessary to peel or core them. Place the apples in a kettle with about 1 inch of water. Cover and cook until soft, stirring occasionally to prevent scorching and to allow the apples to cook evenly.

2   While the apples are cooking, preheat water in your canner. Wash the jars and lids in warm, soapy water and rinse thoroughly. Prepare the lids according to the manufacturer's directions. Put the jars in the canner to warm as you heat the water.

3   When the apples are soft, press through a sieve, strainer, or food mill to remove the skins and seeds.

4   Return the applesauce to a kettle and bring to a boil. Cook for at least 10 minutes, or until the sauce reaches the desired consistency. Season to taste with sugar and cinnamon, if desired.

5   Ladle the hot applesauce into clean, hot jars, leaving ½ inch of headroom. Wipe the rims of the jars with a clean, damp cloth and screw on the lids.

6   Process the jars according to the boiling-water bath canning instructions on page 207 (10 minutes for both pints and quarts; 15 minutes at 1,001–3,000 feet; 20 minutes at 3,001–6,000 feet; and 25 minutes above 6,000 feet).

7   Remove the jars and adjust the screw bands to tighten the seals.

8   Leave the jars undisturbed for 12 hours to cool. Test the seals. Store in a cool, dry place.

Freezing Apples

Even if you select only firm, fresh, and flavorful apples for freezing, you will find that they soften and lose flavor during frozen storage. For that reason, it is important to choose only perfect apples and to refer to the table on page 231 to see which varieties are recommended for freezing. When cooked applesauce is to be frozen, choose those apples listed on the chart as recommended for sauce. Cooking protects the texture and flavor — as long as the sauce is used within a reasonable time.

You can speed up the freezing process somewhat by placing the containers of just-packed fruit on the freezer floor or a shelf and leaving space around each one. When the containers of fruit are completely frozen, repack your freezer to its fullest advantage.

Freezing apple slices or whole apples is a quick way to deal with your harvest. Also, with frozen slices on hand it's so easy to make applesauce at a moment's notice.

FROZEN APPLES

APPLE SLICES

YIELD: 3 quarts

1 Peel, core, and cut 3 pounds (9 medium) apples into ¼-inch slices.

2 Drop into 1 gallon water mixed with 2 tablespoons lemon juice.

3 Bring a pot of water to a boil and drop in the apple slices, a pound at a time. Blanch for 1 minute only. Drain immediately.

4 Place in single layers on baking sheets and freeze.

5 When frozen, place in plastic freezer bags, seal, and freeze.

WHOLE STUFFED APPLES

1 Peel or wash and core the apples.

2 Drop into a pot of boiling water and blanch for 1 minute.

3 Drain and stuff with a mixture of nuts and raisins bound together with honey.

4 Wrap individually in plastic wrap or wax paper. Place in freezer bags and put into the freezer.

5 To prepare the apples for the table, remove from the freezer and place in a buttered dish, dot with butter, cover, and bake in a preheated 400°F oven for 30 minutes, or until they can be pierced easily with a fork.

Freezing Pies

If you intend to freeze baked pies, make sure they are completely cooled before enclosing them in freezer bags. Any heat left in the pie results in condensation in the freezer bag, which causes the pie to become moist and the crust soggy.

Bake frozen prebaked pies in a preheated 375°F oven for approximately 30 minutes, until the filling is hot and juice and steam are visible through the vent. Cover the top with aluminum foil if the crust gets too brown.

Unbaked pies can be assembled as usual, but don't put steam vents in the top crust until you are ready to bake. Bake frozen unbaked pies in a preheated 425°F oven for 30 minutes, then reduce the oven temperature to 375°F and bake for 30 to 40 minutes longer, until the filling is cooked and the crust golden brown. Cover the crust with aluminum foil if it gets too brown before the pie has finished baking.

Making Jams, Jellies, Butters, and Chutneys

Making preserves is simple, economical, and wonderfully satisfying. I get infinite pleasure from surveying jars of golden apple butters, chunky marmalades, and chutneys. And the clear, vivid green of mint-apply jelly is a cause for admiration.

These homemade treasures taste equally good on toast or when accompanying a savory dish.

Of all fruits, tart cooking apples are in a class of their own for jam making because their high pectin content acts as a natural setting agent.

Just for safety, the U.S. Department of Agriculture recommends that all jellies, jams, marmalades, butters, chutneys, and relishes be packed into hot, sterilized jars, leaving ¼ inch of headroom, then sealed according to the jar manufacturer's directions and processed for 5 minutes in a boiling-water bath (or 10 minutes at 1,001–6,000 feet and 15 minutes above 6,000 feet).

STERILIZING JARS AND LIDS

1. **Choose a pan that can be fitted** with a false bottom (such as a plate or a metal rack) to prevent the jars from touching the bottom of the pan and cracking, and one that is deep enough to allow the water to cover the jars.
2. **Wash the jars and lids in warm water** containing a little dishwashing liquid. Rinse thoroughly.
3. **Place the jars upright in the water bath** and fill with hot (not boiling) water. Continue to fill the water bath until the jars are completely covered. Bring to a boil and boil gently for 15 minutes. (Alternatively, some dishwashers have a sterilizing cycle you can use to sterilize jars.)
4. **Scald or boil the lids** according to the manufacturer's directions only.
5. **As the jars are needed for filling,** remove from the boiling water (or dishwasher) one at a time.

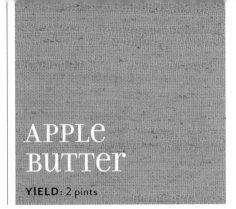

APPLE BUTTER

YIELD: 2 pints

To make this in quantity, quadruple the recipe and cook for several hours. A thick-skinned orange, such as navel or Cara Cara, works well for zesting and juicing.

INGREDIENTS

8–9 medium apples (Paula Red, Golden Delicious, Empire, Idared, McIntosh, Gala), cored and cut into quarters

1 teaspoon water

1 orange

1 pound (2½ cups) brown sugar

1 Place the apples in a large pot, add the water, cover, and cook over low heat for 30 minutes, or until soft. Stir the apples halfway through the cooking time.

2 Grate the zest of the orange and reserve in a small bowl. Cut the orange in half and squeeze the juice into the zest. You should have ½ to ¾ cup juice.

3 Press the cooked apples through a sieve. Discard the skins, return the pulp to the pan, and stir in the brown sugar, grated zest, and orange juice.

4 Cook over very low heat, stirring frequently, until the mixture is thick, about 1½ hours. (Or pour the mixture into a roasting pan and bake uncovered at 350°F for 1 hour, stirring occasionally. Then reduce the oven temperature to 250°F and bake for 2 to 3 hours longer, or until thick.)

5 Sterilize 2 pint jars. Ladle the mixture into the hot, sterilized jars, leaving ¼ inch of headroom. Run a rubber spatula around the inside of the jars to release air bubbles. Wipe the rims of the jars with a clean, damp cloth and screw on the lids. Process for 5 minutes in a boiling-water bath (page 207). Adjust for altitude, if necessary.

APPLE BUTTER FOR PETE

When I was living in Westchester County, New York, environmentalist and folk singer Pete Seeger once asked me to make apple butter at the Clearwater Annual Pumpkin Sail Festival in Beacon, New York. In a letter, he suggested, "We could make the people of the downriver area more conscious of the fact that the Hudson Valley is a great apple-producing region and produces many varieties besides the standard Delicious and Macs." And so we made lots of apple butter near the banks of the Hudson River.

JOYSE'S BLACKBERRY & APPLE JAM

YIELD: about 4 pints

Breakfast at my mother's home in Scotland was never complete without a dish of this jam to accompany the toast. The blackberries grow in wild abundance behind my family's house; in August, you can gather them by the pound.

1   Peel, core, and slice the apples. Reserve the peels. Place the slices in a large kettle with ½ cup of the water. Cover and cook over low heat for 15 to 20 minutes, or until the apples are soft.

2   Place the blackberries in a large saucepan. Add the apple peels, tied in cheesecloth, and the remaining ½ cup water. Cook over low heat for 15 to 20 minutes, or until the fruit is soft.

3   Discard the apple peels. Add the blackberries with their liquid to the apples. (Or force the cooked blackberries through a sieve to remove the seeds; add the fruit pulp to the apples.)

4   Stir in the sugar and dissolve over very low heat.

5   Stir the fruit and bring to a rolling boil over high heat and cook for 10 minutes, or until the jam sets when a spoonful is dropped onto a chilled saucer.

6   When a set has been reached, remove the mixture from the heat and ladle into 4 hot, sterilized pint jars, leaving ¼ inch of headroom. Run a rubber spatula or chopstick around the inside of the jars to release air bubbles. Wipe the rims of the jars with a clean, damp cloth and screw on the lids. Process for 5 minutes in a boiling-water bath (page 207). Adjust for altitude, if necessary.

INGREDIENTS

- 3 medium tart green apples (Granny Smith, Rhode Island Greening, Winesap, Bramley)
- 1 cup water
- 6 cups blackberries
- 8 cups (4 pounds) sugar

I don't remember ever not eating marmalade — it was always served at breakfast. It came in a variety of flavors with thick-cut or finely shredded zest. There was a not-too-tart pure lemon marmalade, but the others were mostly made from oranges, particularly the mildly bitter Seville oranges. Sometimes the marmalades contained crystalized ginger or whisky. All good for slathering on toast or pancakes.

APPLE MARMALADE

YIELD: about 8 pints

INGREDIENTS

- 2 thick-skinned oranges (not thin-skinned juice oranges)
- 2 large lemons
- 1 grapefruit
- 6 medium tart apples (Rhode Island Greening, Granny Smith, Winesap, Bramley)
- 12 cups water
- 5 pounds extra-fine sugar (9 cups)

1 Scrub the oranges, lemons, and grapefruit. Thinly peel the zest with a potato peeler or paring knife, making sure to avoid the inner white pith. Chop or shred the zest. Place in a large stockpot.

2 Cut the ends off the citrus and peel away all the bitter white pith and discard. Pull the fruits in half or cut in half lengthwise. Working over the pot, use a sharp paring knife and cut out the segments of flesh from the membranes. Remove the seeds from the segments and drop the flesh into the pot.

3 Line a medium bowl with a double layer of cheesecloth. Coarsely chop the membranes and place them along with the seeds in the lined bowl. Peel and core the apples. Add the peels and cores to the lined bowl and tie the cheesecloth with kitchen twine to form a bag. Place the bag in the pot and use the twine to tie it to the handle of the pot.

4 Chop the apples and add to the pot; pour in the water. Bring to a boil, reduce the heat, and cook for about 1½ hours, or until the peels are tender and the liquid is reduced by half.

5 Lift the cheesecloth bag above the liquid and use a spoon to press out the juice against the side of the pot. Discard the bag. Add the sugar and stir until completely dissolved. Bring to a boil over high heat and boil rapidly until a candy thermometer registers 220°F, 15 to 20 minutes, or until the marmalade sets when a spoonful is dropped onto a chilled saucer. Skim off the foam.

6 Ladle the mixture into 8 hot, sterilized pint jars, leaving ¼ inch of headroom. Run a rubber spatula or chopstick around the inside of the jars. Wipe the rims of the jars with a clean, damp cloth and screw on the lids. Process for 5 minutes in a boiling-water bath (page 207). Adjust for altitude, if necessary.

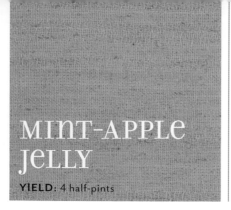

MINT-APPLE JELLY

YIELD: 4 half-pints

For cinnamon-apple jelly, omit the mint leaves and add 2 cinnamon sticks. A few crab apples in the kettle provide extra pectin for a good jelly set.

1 Place the apples in a large kettle with the water and mint. Cook over low heat for 30 minutes, or until the apples are soft.

2 Pour the fruit with its liquid into a sieve or colander lined with four layers of cheesecloth, or into a dampened jelly bag, and strain, allowing it to drip for 2 to 3 hours. For a clear jelly, do not press the fruit.

3 Measure the juice into a clean kettle (there should be about 4 cups) and bring to a boil over high heat. Add the lemon juice and sugar (¾ cup sugar per 1 cup apple juice) and boil for 10 minutes, or until the sugar has dissolved and the jelly registers 220°F on a candy thermometer. The jelly should set when a spoonful is dropped onto a chilled saucer.

4 When the jelly stage has been reached, skim off the foam. Add a drop of green food coloring, if desired.

5 Pour immediately into 4 hot, sterilized half-pint jars, leaving ¼ inch of headroom. Run a rubber spatula or chopstick around the inside of the jars to release air bubbles. Wipe the rims of the jars with a clean, damp cloth and screw on the lids. Process for 5 minutes in a boiling-water bath (page 207). Adjust for altitude, if necessary.

INGREDIENTS

- 10 medium tart apples (Bramley, Granny Smith, Jonathan, Jonagold), cut into quarters
- 3 cups water
- 2 cups fresh mint leaves
- 3 tablespoons lemon juice
- 2¾–3 cups sugar
- Green food coloring (optional)

RHUBARB-APPLE CHUTNEY

YIELD: 7–8 pints

My mother used to make this chutney when she still lived at Woodfalls, her family's farm in Cheshire, England. There was a very large orchard there, and Mother oversaw the making of preserves for home use.

INGREDIENTS

- 5 medium apples (Fuji, Granny Smith, Bramley, Tydeman's Red, Wellington), peeled, cored, and diced
- 4 pounds rhubarb, cut into 1-inch pieces
- 4 medium onions, chopped
- 1 pound raisins
- 1 pound brown sugar
- 2½ cups malt vinegar
- 2 teaspoons curry powder
- ½ teaspoon ground cinnamon
- ½ teaspoon ground cloves
- ½ teaspoon ground ginger
- ½ teaspoon freshly grated or ground nutmeg

1 Combine the apples, rhubarb, onions, raisins, brown sugar, vinegar, curry powder, cinnamon, cloves, ginger, and nutmeg in a large kettle, cover, and bring to a boil over high heat.

2 Remove the lid, reduce the heat to very low, and cook for approximately 2 hours, or until the chutney is thick and tender.

3 Ladle into 7 or 8 hot, sterilized pint jars, leaving ¼ inch of headroom. Run a rubber spatula or chopstick around the inside of the jars to release air bubbles. Wipe the rims of the jars with a clean, damp cloth and screw on the lids. Process for 5 minutes in a boiling-water bath (page 207). Adjust for altitude, if necessary.

CHAPTER 8

Meet the Apples: Apple Varieties

DESCRIPTIONS OF THE GENERAL CHARACTERISTICS of apples should be taken as just that — general. Like that of wines, the quality of apples depends on many factors — latitude, terrain, weather, and the care with which they are grown, among others. Apples of the same variety vary not only from year to year but also from day to day as they mature.

I've had apples from the same bag, in fact, that varied widely in appearance and taste. Maybe they were the same shape, but the colors were remarkably different, depending on the degree of ripeness.

The background, or undercast, color of an apple changes from dark green to light green to yellow as it ripens, and the surface turns a bright red or a deeper yellow. In some apples, the surface color completely obscures the background color. Take, for example, one of my favorite apples, the Empire. Sometimes it is all bright red, other times bright red on a yellow background. A knockout of juicy spiciness when fully mature, the Empire is flat and uninteresting when eaten before its prime.

Some apples at first look are only a solid green, yellow, or red, but, on closer inspection, it can often be seen that they are faintly streaked, marbled, or dotted with a yellow or pink blush. Get to know the apples — from everyday varieties to heirlooms to new hybrids — in the following pages.

Popular Varieties

The following descriptions cover those apple varieties that are the most popular with the orchardists, are good keepers, and are available for several months in a number of U.S. states and Canadian provinces.

BRAEBURN. Discovered as a seedling in New Zealand in 1952, it is believed to be an offspring of the Lady Hamilton. A yellow-skinned apple blushed with red stripes, Braeburn has pale cream flesh that is crisp, juicy, and sweetly tart. A favorite apple for fresh desserts, it is also good for baking and making into a deliciously sweet applesauce.

CAMEO. Discovered in the 1980s as a chance seedling in a Golden and Red Delicious orchard in the Wenatchee River Valley, Washington, it was released on the market in 1987. It is a large apple with yellow- and red-striped or spotted skin. The flavorful flesh is crisp, juicy, and sweet-tart, making it a good

Braeburn

Cameo

keeper and all-purpose apple. The dense, cream-colored flesh also resists browning, so it is an ideal contender for salads and fruit plates.

CORTLAND. This apple, a cross between a Ben Davis and a McIntosh, was developed by the New York State Agricultural Experiment Station in Geneva, New York. It entered the commercial market in 1915. Cortlands are grown mainly in the Northeast, the northern Great Lakes states, and eastern Canada. A medium-to-large red-and-green-striped apple, it is crisp, juicy, and sweetly tart. Because its white flesh resists browning, Cortland is favored for salads and fruit cups. It is also a good all-purpose apple.

FORTUNE. Developed by the Cornell University New York State Agricultural Experiment Station in 1996 as a cross between Empire and Red Spy, it resembles both with its tender red skin and spicy sweet-tart flavor. A larger apple with crisp cream-colored flesh, the Fortune has all the qualities of a great all-purpose apple for baking, cooking, salads, and eating out of hand.

FUJI. This flavorful, aromatic apple is the number-one seller in Japan, where it was developed in 1958 by crossing the Ralls Genet and Red Delicious. A pretty apple with yellowish-green skin blushed with orange red stripes, it has dense, crisp, and sweetly tart light yellow flesh. Fuji retains its flavor even when stored at room temperature and develops a better flavor when held in long-term storage. An excellent apple for eating out of hand, adding to salads, and making into applesauce.

GALA. Developed in 1934 in New Zealand by J. H. Kidd of Greytown, Wairarapa, Gala (sometimes called Royal Gala) is a cross of Kidd's Orange Red and Golden Delicious. The thin, red-orange skin — actually red striping over gold — encases aromatic, semisweet, yellowish-white flesh. Crisp and juicy, it is a good apple for eating out of hand, using in salads, and pairing with soft, mild cheeses.

GINGER GOLD. Ginger Gold was discovered as a seedling in an orchard in Virginia after Hurricane Camille devastated the area in 1969. It is believed to be the offspring of Albemarle Pippin. It is a large apple with greenish-gold skin, which is sometimes tinged with a slight blush when fully mature. The crisp, juicy flesh is pure white and resists turning brown for hours after it has been peeled and cut. This combination makes Ginger Gold a good choice for salads, hors d'oeuvre trays, and garnishes.

Cortland   Fuji   Gala   Ginger Gold

When the apple is first picked, its flavor is tart with a sweet aftertaste, but as it matures under refrigeration, its flesh becomes mellow and honey sweet. Ginger Gold is best eaten within two months of harvest.

GOLDEN DELICIOUS. Grown in most regions across the country, Golden Delicious is the second-most grown after Red Delicious, to which it is not at all related. The Golden Delicious (or Yellow Delicious, as it is sometimes called) was discovered in West Virginia in 1914, when it was called Mullin's Yellow Seedling. Stark Bro's Nursery, in Louisiana, Missouri, which specializes in acquiring the rights to new apple varieties, later acquired the Golden Delicious. Sometimes, the nursery has found new varieties through fruit competitions it sponsored. This is a medium-to-large pale yellow or yellow-green apple that is mild and sweet. Although it is crisp when harvested in September and October, its pale flesh often becomes dry and soft. Its skin shrivels when not refrigerated. Particularly desirable for snacks, fresh desserts, and salads, the Golden Delicious is a good all-purpose apple.

GRANNY SMITH. Although one of the most popular varieties sold in the United States, it is imported here year-round from the Southern Hemisphere. Granny Smith originated in Sydney, Australia, about 100 years ago and is now grown in several states. It is a medium pale green apple that, depending on maturity, is mildly to very tart. It is crisp and firm, and even though it doesn't have great flavor, its rather hard flesh makes it a good all-purpose apple. The U.S. crop is available from October through June.

HONEYCRISP. A cross between Macoun and Honeygold, this outstanding keeper was developed at the University of Minnesota in 1991. This is a large apple with red-and-yellow-striped tender skin encasing superbly crisp, sweet-tart, honeyed flesh dripping with juice. This apple has nudged Red Delicious lower on the rung, and for many consumers Honeycrisp is their number-one choice for snacking and salads. It is also excellent for sauce and as an all-purpose cooking apple.

IDARED. This apple was scientifically developed in 1942 at the University of Idaho

Golden Delicious   Granny Smith   Honeycrisp

Agricultural Experiment Station. It is a cross between a Jonathan and a Wagener. Although it is grown in greatest volume in the Northeast and Upper Midwest, its production is increasing by popular demand throughout the country. It is medium to large and bright red, and it has creamy white flesh that is very firm, crisp, and juicy. All-purpose apples, the sweetly tart, deliciously spicy Idareds are especially good for snacks and desserts, and their firm quality makes them particularly desirable for baking. The flavor improves after several months in controlled-atmosphere storage.

JAZZ. The trade name for Scifresh, a variety developed in New Zealand, this Braeburn–Royal Gala cross was first planted in Washington State by the McDougall family in 2004 and is now ranked as one of the top 10 apples. Tangy-sweet and crisp, this red-splashed-with-yellow apple retains its crunch for a long time, making it an exceptional keeper. It is great apple for the lunch box and salads, and its flavor and texture also hold up in cooked and baked dishes.

JERSEYMAC. This is a medium-to-large red apple with a green undercast. Its tough skin encases flesh that is tangy, crunchy, and juicy. Although it makes a good all-purpose apple, it does not keep well.

JONAGOLD. The Cornell University New York State Agricultural Experiment Station developed the Jonagold by crossing Jonathan and Golden Delicious. It was introduced to American consumers in 1968. A large, slightly elliptical apple with red skin or yellow skin blushed with faint orange-red stripes, it has flesh that is supercrisp, juicy, and an even balance of sweet and tart. Jonagold is an excellent all-purpose apple, one of the best for eating out of hand.

JONAMAC. A small-to-medium, red-on-green apple that is firm, mildly tart, and juicy, it can be considered an all-purpose apple. However, it is not a good keeper.

MACOUN. A cross between a McIntosh and a Jersey Black, this is a medium red apple that sometimes has an unattractive gray bloom. However, its snow-white flesh is supercrisp and juicy, and its honey sweetness makes up for its mild flavor.

Jazz   Jonagold   Macoun

McINTOSH. John McIntosh discovered this apple in Ontario, Canada, in 1830. Ranking third in volume in the United States, it is grown throughout the Northeast, the northern Great Lakes states, eastern Canada, and British Columbia. It is a medium red-on-green apple, with sweet flesh that is crisp, juicy, and slightly perfumed. Macs are excellent to eat fresh in autumn; later, they are best used for sauce. McIntosh apples collapse when baked whole or in pies.

MELROSE. In 1970, the Ohio State Horticultural Society named Melrose the official state apple. It has a somewhat flat shape, and the skin is a dull red on yellow. However, it makes up for its drab appearance with firm, crisp flesh that is sweet, juicy, and flavorful. Melrose is an excellent all-purpose apple.

MUTSU/CRISPIN. This descendant of Golden Delicious was introduced into the United States by the Japanese in 1948. Although grown mostly in the Northeast, Mutsu is gaining wider popularity. The very large yellow-green fruit is not unlike the Golden Delicious; however, the flesh is much juicier and coarser, and its skin suffers less from storage. It is an excellent all-purpose apple.

PATRICIA. A star, this is so limited in production that it sells out very quickly during the second week of September. One of the very best eaters, but not a good keeper, it is a small, light green and yellow apple splashed with pink. It is crisp, crunchy, juicy, and sweet and tastes of "apple."

PAULA RED. This variety was discovered in 1960 in Sparta, Michigan, and introduced commercially in 1967. It is grown mostly in the Northeast and northern Midwest states. A medium, early-September apple, it is usually red, though sometimes shaded with yellow-green. The flesh is crisp, juicy, and sweetly tart. Although Paula Reds are fair all-purpose apples, they are not good keepers and should be used within six weeks or so of harvest.

PINK LADY (aka CRIPPS PINK). This intensely flavored sweet-tart apple with its bright pink skin flecked with yellow-green was developed in Australia in the 1980s as a hybrid cross of Golden Delicious and Lady Williams. An all-purpose apple when fresh, its flesh turns amazingly sweet during long-term storage and is then best for salads, fruit plates, snacking, and in sauce.

McIntosh

Mutsu/Crispin

Paula Red

RARITAN. This red-on-green apple has a great "apple" flavor and is one of my all-time favorites. It has wondrously crunchy, juice-spurting flesh that is mildly tart-sweet. It is a great thirst quencher.

RED DELICIOUS. The Red Delicious is grown throughout the United States and is still America's most popularly grown apple. It was called Hawkeye when it was discovered in 1872 in Peru, Iowa, and was renamed Delicious in 1895 by the Stark Bro's Nursery. (George Stark is said to have proclaimed, "It's delicious," when he took a bite of Jesse Hiatt's Hawkeye during the judging of the Stark's 1892 apple competition. The Stark Nurseries bought the rights for Hawkeye from Hiatt and first called it Stark Delicious.) This bright red apple is crisp and juicy when harvested in September and October. Although Red Delicious is considered a good keeper by the industry, its sweet and mild-tasting flesh is all too often a mealy, mushy disappointment. It is best used for snacks, salads, and fruit cups.

ROME BEAUTY. This large deep red apple was found growing in Rome, Ohio, in 1816. The flesh is sweet, mildly tart, dry, and firm. Although mediocre for eating fresh, Rome Beauty is very good for baking because it retains its shape and flavor. For that reason it remains one of the most popular varieties grown throughout the United States.

STAYMAN. Stayman apples were discovered in Leavenworth, Kansas, in 1866 and originated from Winesap seeds. For that reason, they are sometimes incorrectly called Stayman Winesap. They're grown in the Northeast, eastern Midwest, and South Atlantic states. Stayman is a medium deep red apple, often shaded with green (it sometimes fails to ripen in the Northeast). Its sweetly tart flesh is crisp and juicy and is delicious for eating fresh. It is also a good all-purpose apple.

WINESAP. Thought to have originated in New Jersey in the late 1700s, Winesap is one of our oldest apples still in commercial production (Newtown Pippin is the other). Although it is grown in most apple-producing regions, its heaviest volume comes from the Northwest and the Mid-Atlantic states. The Winesap is of medium size, with a thick red skin and crisp, crunchy, juicy flesh. The flavor is sweetly tart with a winey aftertaste. It is an excellent all-purpose apple.

Pink Lady   Red Delicious   Winesap

YORK IMPERIAL. When this apple was first discovered at York, Pennsylvania, around 1830, it was called Johnson's Fine Winter Apple. It is grown in the Appalachian states of Pennsylvania, West Virginia, Virginia, Maryland, and Delaware, and its production volume is high enough to rank sixth in the United States. An apple of medium size with a lopsided shape, it has deep red skin with greenish-yellow streaking. York Imperial is a crisp, firm apple that is both sweet and tart, with a somewhat mild flavor, and it is in great demand for commercial processing into pie filling and sauce. It is a good all-purpose apple that mellows in cold storage.

Hardy Heirloom Apple Varieties

Thousands of apple varieties evolved in the United States during the seventeenth, eighteenth, and nineteenth centuries when Colonial farmers decided to plant apple seeds instead of the young apple tree shoots, or scions, that were transported from England and the Continent. It was thus they found that the seed of an apple did not produce a tree of the same original variety. It was also during the eighteenth and nineteenth centuries that apple seeds were spread from coast to coast by the legendary Johnny Appleseed. Born John Chapman in 1774 in Massachusetts, he traveled the new territories for 40-odd years, selling seeds, cuttings, and plants.

The demise of certain apple strains was inevitable. With thousands of varieties to be eaten and sold, those that spoiled quickly were considered a bad risk. By the turn of the twentieth century, when transportation became more reliable and all manner of food was available from different areas of the country and various parts of the globe, the heavy reliance on homegrown and local food was drastically diminished. No longer was the home orchard the main source of fruit. Consequently, it was no longer practical to grow such a wide variety of apple trees. Only those that produced apples judged to be good keepers and the best for making pies, sauce, and cider were cultivated. Apples that could not stand up to shipping and long storage were discontinued, as were trees that did not bear their first crop for 10 years, and then only every other year thereafter. Also neglected were those apples with rough, brownish, or mottled skins, deemed to be aesthetically unacceptable to the American public.

Another important element contributed to the elimination of some apple varieties. In 1918, the ravages of a severe winter took their toll on thousands of apple trees in the East. In starting over, commercial orchard growers followed the recommendations of pomologists and planted an abundance of McIntosh, Red Delicious, Golden Delicious, and Rome Beauties. However, such old-time favorites as Wealthy, Tolman Sweet, Pound Sweet, Rhode Island Greening, and Baldwin can still be found in some of the smaller commercial orchards whose clientele is local rather than nationwide.

Indeed, I consider it a lucky day when I stumble upon an old-fashioned orchard, where the gardener prefers flavor to abundance. Such varieties can be a revelation — not only in taste but also in name and appearance.

ASHMEAD'S KERNEL. This apple was grown around 1700 by Dr. Ashmead in Gloucester, England. Considered one of the finest dessert apples, it has a sugary sweetness that is deliciously tempered by a touch of acid in the juice. Adding to this wonderful flavor, the slightly green, yellow flesh is crisp and aromatic. Ashmeads, somewhat lopsided and conical in shape, have golden-bronze russet skin blushed with orange.

BALDWIN. This apple originated in Wilmington, Massachusetts, around 1740. Grown mostly in New York State and New England, it is no longer popular with commercial growers because it takes about 10 years to bear fruit, and then does so only biennially. It is a large red apple, streaked with yellow. The flesh is firm, crisp, juicy, moderately tart, and aromatic. This is a good all-purpose apple.

BLACK GILLIFLOWER OR SHEEPNOSE. This apple, discovered in Connecticut in the late 1700s, has the shape of a sheep's nose and deep purple-red skin. The flesh is firm, sweet, and fragrant. It is delicious for eating out of hand and can also be used for baking.

BLACK TWIG. Sometimes spelled Blacktwig, this apple is also known as Twitty's Paragon. Discovered as a seedling around 1830 on the farm of Major Rankin Toole in Fayetteville, Tennessee, it was distributed by Twitty's nursery. In the nineteenth and early twentieth centuries, Black Twig was a popular variety with orchardists in central Virginia. Considered a good keeper, this juicy and aromatic apple needs some storage time for its yellow flesh to develop the best flavor. The attractive skin is usually yellow striped and blushed with dark red.

CHENANGO STRAWBERRY. This originated in New York State in the mid-1800s and is a pale yellow apple with pink stripes. The soft flesh has a distinctive strawberry fragrance.

COX ORANGE PIPPIN. *Pippin* was a common term for a small apple when this one originated in England around 1830. It is wonderfully aromatic, with a rather rough, deep yellow skin that is splashed with orange and red. The flesh is crisp, tender, and fragrantly juicy, making it one of the best dessert apples. It also makes choice cider.

Ashmead's Kernel   Baldwin   Black Gilliflower

DUCHESS OF OLDENBURG. First imported to England in 1815 from Russia, this apple was brought to the United States in 1835. Its tender, red-striped skin encases yellow-tinged flesh. Crisp, firm, and juicy, it is highly rated for pies and sauces but considered too tart for eating out of hand.

FAMEUSE OR SNOW. Originating in France, this has been grown in New York and Vermont since around 1700. It is small and firm, with bright red, sometimes purple, skin. Its snow-white, crisp flesh may be striped with red. Excellent for eating raw in desserts and salads, it does not hold its shape during cooking.

JONATHAN. This was called a Rick apple when it was first introduced in 1826 at Woodstock, New York. Although it represents the fifth-largest apple crop in the United States, its production in the North is now limited. It is a medium red apple with an attractive yellow blush. The flesh is firm, crisp, juicy, and sweetly tart, with a spicy aftertaste. A great all-purpose apple that holds its shape well, Jonathan is in demand for baking whole and in pies.

LADY. This small apple originated in France during medieval times. With its red and green skin and firm, crisp, white flesh, it is very much in demand around the Christmas season for table decorations. It is delicious to eat fresh and makes good cider. It is not related to the much larger Pink Lady.

NEWTOWN PIPPIN. Supposedly discovered in Newtown, New York, on Long Island, in 1758, this is one of the oldest varieties to be found in commercial production. It is now grown in several states and is a great favorite with the processing industry — its firm, crisp, juicy, and sweetly tart flesh makes it ideal for pie fillings and sauce.

NORTHERN SPY. This apple originated at East Bloomfield, New York, around 1800. Today, it is grown mostly throughout the Northeast, the northern Midwest, and eastern Canada. This is a medium-to-large apple with a pale green to yellow undercast, heavily striped with red. Its mellow, creamy flesh is crisp, juicy, and richly aromatic — qualities that are prized by the commercial processing industry. It is an excellent all-purpose apple and freezes well. Because it is a biennial bearer, Northern Spy is declining in popularity with commercial orchardists.

Cox Orange Pippin

Lady

Northern Spy

PORTER. A large yellow apple splashed with red, it originated in Massachusetts around 1800. Its firm white flesh is crisp, tender, and flavorful. It is ideal for canning, cooking, and eating raw.

POUND SWEET OR PUMPKIN SWEET. This apple originated in Connecticut around 1850. It is very large, with green-on-yellow striped skin. The flesh is yellow and juicy, with an unusual and rather sweet flavor. It is good for baking.

RED ASTRACHAN. This apple reached the United States from Russia around 1835. Its pale yellow skin is splashed with bluish-red stripes, and the juicy white flesh is often tinged with red. An early-summer apple that ripens unevenly and does not keep well, the Red Astrachan is used for cooking before it is fully mature. However, when ripe, it is excellent for eating fresh in desserts and salads.

RHODE ISLAND GREENING. This variety originated around 1700 from a chance seedling found growing outside a Rhode Island tavern owned by a Mr. Green of Green's End, Newport. The bright green skin surrounds flesh that is crisp, juicy, and tart. If allowed to ripen, it becomes mellow enough to be eaten out of hand. However, most orchardists pick it "green," which makes it a perfect pie apple.

ROXBURY RUSSET. A real American oldie that originated in Roxbury, Massachusetts, around 1635. Its gold skin is mottled with flecks of brown and red; the crisp yellow flesh is deliciously sweet. Excellent for eating fresh and making into cider, it also has a long storage life.

SMOKEHOUSE. William Gibbons grew this apple near his smokehouse during the early nineteenth century in Lancaster County, Pennsylvania. Its yellowish-green skin is mottled with red and the creamy flesh is firm and juicy, making it a good candidate for fresh desserts and the salad bowl. It is not recommended for cooking.

SOPS OF WINE. With red-flecked white flesh that resembles bread dipped in wine, this apple has a pedigree that goes all the way back to medieval England.

Pound Sweet

Rhode Island Greening

Roxbury Russet

SUMMER RAMBO. One of the older varieties, it originated in France, where it was called the Rambour Franc, and was introduced into the United States in 1817. This large apple is greenish yellow with red stripes. The tender, juicy flesh makes it ideal for eating fresh and making into sauce.

TOLMAN SWEET. This apple is said to have originated in Dorchester, Massachusetts, around 1822. Its greenish-yellow skin is sometimes blushed with light pink. The white flesh is exceptionally sweet, and it is considered the best for making naturally sweet applesauce. It is also good for baking and eating fresh.

TOMPKINS KING. Discovered in New Jersey around 1800, it is a large yellow apple splashed with broad red stripes. The skin is tender and the creamy flesh crisp, juicy, and moderately tart. Not a favorite for eating fresh, it is best used for cooking.

TWENTY OUNCE. It was first exhibited in Massachusetts around 1845 and is thought to have originated in Connecticut. This is a large green apple splashed with red stripes when ripe. Its firm, tart flesh is encased in tough skin. This combination makes it superb for cooking.

WEALTHY. This thin-skinned, pale yellow apple, heavily shaded with red, was discovered in Minnesota around 1860. Its crisp, juicy white flesh is often streaked with red. It's an excellent apple for eating fresh, for cooking, and for making cider.

WESTFIELD SEEK-NO-FURTHER. At one time considered the finest of dessert apples, this one originated in Westfield, Massachusetts, around 1796. The skin of this yellowish-green apple is splashed with red, and the pale yellow flesh is crisp, juicy, and flavorful.

WINTER BANANA. Over 100 years old, this variety originated in Indiana. It has pink-on-yellow cheeks and, not surprisingly, a flavor reminiscent of bananas.

WOLF RIVER. Named after the Wolf River in Wisconsin, where it was found, this apple is thought to have originated in 1880. It is an oversized apple, and stories abound in which only one apple was necessary for a whole pie. Its skin is pale yellow, heavily streaked with red, and the light yellow flesh is firm, tender, and juicy. It's excellent for eating fresh and cooking.

Westfield Seek-No-Further

Winter Banana

APPLE VARIETIES AND THEIR BEST USES

Best Apples for EATING

EXCELLENT: Ashmead's Kernel, Black Gilliflower, Braeburn, Cameo, Fameuse, Fortune, Fuji, Honeycrisp, Jazz, Jonagold, Jonathan, Lady, Macoun, Mutsu/Crispin, Patricia, Pink Lady, Porter, Raritan, Roxbury Russet, Summer Rambo, Wealthy, Winesap, Wolf River, York Imperial

GOOD: Baldwin, Black Twig, Chenango Strawberry, Cortland, Gala, Ginger Gold, Golden Delicious, Granny Smith, Idared, Jerseymac, Jonamac, McIntosh, Melrose, Newtown Pippin, Northern Spy, Paula Red, Red Delicious, Stayman, Tolman Sweet

Best Apples for SALAD

EXCELLENT: Ashmead's Kernel, Braeburn, Cameo, Cortland, Fameuse, Fortune, Fuji, Ginger Gold, Golden Delicious, Honeycrisp, Jazz, Jonagold, Red Astrachan, Smokehouse, Winesap

GOOD: Baldwin, Black Twig, Gala, Granny Smith, Idared, Jerseymac, Jonamac, Jonathan, Macoun, Melrose, Mutsu/Crispin, Newtown Pippin, Northern Spy, Patricia, Paula Red, Pink Lady, Raritan, Red Delicious, Stayman, York Imperial

Best Apples for SAUCE

EXCELLENT: Braeburn, Duchess of Oldenburg, Fortune, Fuji, Gala, Golden Delicious, Honeycrisp, Jonathan, Melrose, Mutsu/Crispin, Newtown Pippin, Summer Rambo, Tolman Sweet, Winesap, York Imperial

GOOD: Baldwin, Cameo, Cortland, Ginger Gold, Idared, Jazz, Jerseymac, Jonagold, Jonamac, Macoun, McIntosh, Northern Spy, Patricia, Paula Red, Pink Lady, Raritan, Rhode Island Greening, Rome Beauty, Stayman, Twenty Ounce

Best Apples for BAKING WHOLE

EXCELLENT: Braeburn, Cox Orange Pippin, Fortune, Honeycrisp, Idared, Jonathan, Melrose, Northern Spy, York Imperial

GOOD: Baldwin, Cameo, Cortland, Gala, Ginger Gold, Golden Delicious, Granny Smith, Jazz, Jonagold, Mutsu/Crispin, Newtown Pippin, Rhode Island Greening, Rome Beauty, Stayman, Tolman Sweet, Twenty Ounce, Winesap

Best Apples for PIE

EXCELLENT: Braeburn, Cox Orange Pippin, Duchess of Oldenburg, Fortune, Honeycrisp, Idared, Jonathan, Melrose, Mutsu/Crispin, Newtown Pippin, Northern Spy, Porter, York Imperial

GOOD: Baldwin, Black Gilliflower, Cameo, Cortland, Fuji, Gala, Ginger Gold, Golden Delicious, Granny Smith, Jazz, Jonagold, Pound Sweet, Rhode Island Greening, Rome Beauty, Stayman, Tompkins King, Twenty Ounce, Winesap

Best Apples for FREEZING

EXCELLENT: Melrose, Northern Spy

GOOD: Braeburn, Cameo, Fortune, Golden Delicious, Granny Smith, Honeycrisp, Idared, Jazz, Jonagold, Jonathan, Mutsu/Crispin, Newtown Pippin, Porter, Rhode Island Greening, Rome Beauty, Stayman, Twenty Ounce, Winesap, York Imperial

Appendixes

Apple Information and Sources

U.S. Apple Association
703-442-8850
www.usapple.org

The links page provides contact information for U.S. state and regional apple organizations.

NOTE: The U.S. Apple Association (formerly the International Apple Institute), based in Vienna, Virginia, is the national trade association representing all segments of the apple industry, including orchardists located throughout the country.

Experimental Orchards

These orchards are among those producing new hybrid and/or heirloom apple varieties.

Breezy Hill Orchard and Cider Mill
828 Centre Road
Staatsburg, NY 12580
845-266-3979
www.hudsonvalleycider.com

Distillery Lane Ciderworks
5533 Gapland Road
Jefferson, MD 21755
301-834-8920
http://distillerylaneciderworks.com

Doud Orchards
8971 North State Road 19
Denver, IN 46926
765-985-3937

Started in 1894, Doud Orchards (now owned by the Shanley family) is considered an Indiana landmark. The orchard of 9,000 trees features 150 apple varieties, including many antiques. Visitors can learn about and taste the antique varieties.

Hollabaugh Bros., Inc.
545 Carlisle Road
Biglerville, PA 17307
717-677-8412
www.hollabaughbros.com

Salinger's Orchard
230 Guinea Road
Brewster, NY 10509
845-277-3521
http://salingersorchard.com

Metric Conversion Charts

Unless you have finely calibrated measuring equipment, conversions between U.S. and metric measurements will be inexact. It's important to convert the measurements for all the ingredients in a recipe to maintain the same proportions as the original.

General Formula for Metric Conversion

Ounces to grams	multiply ounces by 28.35
Grams to ounces	multiply grams by 0.035
Pounds to grams	multiply pounds by 453.5
Pounds to kilograms	multiply pounds by 0.45
Cups to liters	multiply cups by 0.24
Fahrenheit to Celsius	subtract 32 from Fahrenheit temperature, multiply by 5, then divide by 9
Celsius to Fahrenheit	multiply Celsius temperature by 9, divide by 5, then add 32

Approximate Metric Equivalents by Volume

U.S.	Metric
1 teaspoon	5 milliliters
1 tablespoon	15 milliliters
⅓ cup	60 milliliters
½ cup	120 milliliters
1 cup	230 milliliters
1¼ cups	300 milliliters
1½ cups	360 milliliters
2 cups	460 milliliters
2½ cups	600 milliliters
3 cups	700 milliliters
4 cups (1 quart)	0.95 liter
1.06 quarts	1 liter
4 quarts (1 gallon)	3.8 liters

Approximate Metric Equivalents by Weight

U.S.	Metric	Metric	U.S.
¼ ounce	7 grams	1 gram	0.035 ounce
½ ounce	14 grams	50 grams	1.75 ounces
1 ounce	28 grams	100 grams	3.5 ounces
1¼ ounces	35 grams	250 grams	8.75 ounces
1½ ounces	40 grams	500 grams	1.1 pounds
2½ ounces	70 grams	1 kilogram	2.2 pounds
4 ounces	112 grams		
5 ounces	140 grams		
8 ounces	228 grams		
10 ounces	280 grams		
15 ounces	425 grams		
16 ounces (1 pound)	454 grams		

Acknowledgments

The Apple Cookbook is an homage to pomologists (breeders) and orchardists all over the world. Perhaps particular thanks go to the orchardists who plant, nurture, prune, and — despite the setbacks caused sometimes by heavy frosts at spring bloomtime or unpredictable invasions of insects — manage to produce crops of wonderful apples. I marvel at always finding such a great variety, and I know that new ones are being bred and discovered all the time.

There are so many people who made this book possible that I cannot mention them all — indeed, some of them work behind the scenes at Storey Publishing and are never known to me, but special thanks go to:

Margaret Sutherland, acquisitions editor at Storey Publishing, and key editor who guided my way through this updated edition of *The Apple Cookbook*, which, when it was first published in 1984, won a Tastemaker Award, now known as the James Beard Foundation Award.

Mike Ashby, the copy editor who pushed me to clarify throughout and make the recipe directions accessible to eighth graders.

Art director Mary Velgos; photographers Leigh Beisch, Stacey Cramp, and Mars Vilaubi; and food stylists Robyn Valarik and Vanessa Seder, whose work added beautiful visual appeal to my recipes. And everyone else at Storey who had a hand in this new edition.

The orchards that allowed Stacey Cramp to photograph their trees and fruit: Sweetser's Apple Barrel and Orchards, Cumberland, Maine; Randall Orchards, Standish, Maine; Super Chilly Farm, Palermo, Maine; Sandy River Apples, Mercer, Maine; School House Farm, Warren, Maine; and Lost Nation Orchard, Groveton, N.H.

Former Storey president and current Workman CEO Dan Reynolds, who has spearheaded the marketing of Storey books for decades, and Maribeth Casey of international sales, who has handled the foreign translations of several of my cookbooks.

Julia Stewart of Clarity Communications and the spokesperson for the New York Apple Association, who was always there to answer questions about apples and the apple industry.

Wendy Brannen, director, consumer health and public relations of the U.S. Apple Association in Vienna, Virginia, who helped me update production figures and facts.

Dr. Susan Brown, head pomologist at Cornell University's Department of Horticultural Sciences at the New York State Agricultural Station in Geneva, New York, who steered me through the complicated issue of germplasm and the process of breeding hybrid apples.

And my friends, family, colleagues, and orchardists, who shared recipes and knowledge of apples.

Index

Page numbers in *italic* indicate photos; page numbers in **bold** indicate charts.

A

Acorn Squash with Rice, Apple & Pecan Stuffing, 87
almonds/almond paste
    Almond-Apple Streusel, 150
    Apple, Dried Fruit & Israeli Couscous Salad, 74
    Sherried Apple Crêpes, 187
antioxidants, 77
apple(s), 220–231. *See also* preserving apples
    allure of, 9–10
    antioxidants and, 77
    breeding programs, 11–15, 83
    buying, 15–17
    characteristics of, 220
    cooking with, 17–18, 94
    equivalents, **17**
    food processor and, 18
    freezing, 206, 210, *210*, 231
    grades of, 16
    heirloom varieties, 13–14, 226–230
    history of, 8–9
    hybrids, new, 11–13
    keeping from browning, 73
    in low-fat baking, 154
    nutritional value, raw, 72
    peeling/not peeling, 17
    popular varieties, 10–11, 147, 147, 220–26
    statistics on, 125
    storage of, 18–19
    substituting varieties, 19
    uses for, best, 231
apple, cheese, and wine party, 62
apple cider, 23, 52. *See also* apple juice or cider; sparkling cider/wine
    Apple Cider Sidecar, The, 56
    Calvados & Cider Soufflé, 190, *191*
    Turkey Scaloppini with Apple Cider and Mushrooms, 118
apple juice or cider
    Apple-Date Cream Cheese Spread, 49
    Apple Eggnog, 57
    Apple Sorbet, 194
    Fall Fruit Relish, 98
    Iced Apple Tea, 52

    Party Apple Punch, 56
    Pork Tenderloin with Apple-Shallot Sauce, 120
    Sweet Applesauce, 176
    Triple Apple, Fruit & Veg Shake, 53
apple-picking tips, 138, *138*
applesauce
    Apple-Cinnamon Soufflé, 193
    Apple Fool, 194
    Apple Maple Sauce, 34
    Applesauce & Whole-Wheat Yeast Rolls, 48
    Applesauce Brownies, 200
    Applesauce Gingerbread, 165
    Applesauce Muffins, 45
    Apple Sorbet, 194
    Bran-Applesauce Muffins, 44
    Canned Applesauce, 209
    Chocolate-Applesauce Cake, 164
    Granola, Applesauce & Yogurt Sundae, 23
    Louise Salinger's Apple Meat Loaf, 130, *131*
    Oatmeal-Apple Cupcakes, 169
    Pork Tenderloin with Apple-Shallot Sauce, 120
    Sweet Applesauce, 176
    Triple Apple, Fruit & Veg Shake, 53
    Unsweetened Applesauce, 80, *80*
    Whole-Wheat & Nut Quick Bread, 40
apple slices, canned
    Apple-Cheddar Crêpes, 29
    Baked Apples & Cheese, 106
    Breakfast Sausage Crêpes, 28
    Canned Apple Slices, 208
Apricot-Apple Dumplings, 202
Apricot Cobbler, Apple-, 182, *183*
Apricot Cream Cheese Spread, 49
Ashmead's Kernel, 227, *227*
Autumn Crisp, 12
avocados
    Avocado & Apple Composed Salad with Buttermilk-Herb Dressing, 68, *69*
    Triple Apple, Fruit & Veg Shake, 53

B

bacon
    Apple & Sausage Bundles, 59
    Potato-Apple Salad, 78, *79*
    Spinach with Leek, Bacon & Apple, 81
baking whole, best apples for, 231
Baldwin, 227, *227*
Balsamic-Herb Dressing, 70
bananas
    Apple-Banana Bread, 38
    Fresh Apple & Mango Smoothie, 54, *55*
    Triple Apple, Fruit & Veg Shake, 53
Barbara Mullin's Apple Cobbler, 181
Barbara Mullin's Coffee Can Bread, 41
Bean Soup, Black, 104
beef
    Beef & Apple Deep-Dish Pie, 128
    Curried Apple Meat Loaf, 129
    Louise Salinger's Apple Meat Loaf, 130, *131*
beets
    Apple, Pear & Beet Composed Salad with Balsamic-Herb Dressing, 70
bell peppers
    Apple & Red Bell Pepper Stuffing Balls, 92
    Apple Frittata, 27
    Apple Ratatouille, 86
Black Bean Soup, 104
Blackberry & Apple Jam, Joyse's, 214
Blackberry Crisp, Apple-, 178, *179*
Black Gilliflower, 227, *227*
Black Twig, 227
boiling-water bath canning, 207, *207*
Bourbon Cake, New York Apple-, 166, *167*
Braeburn, 220, *220*
Bran-Applesauce Muffins, 44
bread. *See also* stuffing
    Apple, Sausage & Cheese Strata, 90, *91*

bread *(continued)*
  Apple-Banana Bread, 38
  Apple Rarebit Supper, 105
  Barbara Mullin's Coffee Can
    Bread, 41
  Chicken & Apple Gyros, 114,
    115
  Louise Salinger's Apple Meat
    Loaf, 130, *131*
  Louse Salinger's Apple Tea
    Bread, 39
  Microwave Apple Bread Pud-
    ding, 197
  Pork Tenderloin Stuffed with
    Apples, 122, *123*
  Whole-Wheat & Nut Quick
    Bread, 40
Breezy Hill Hard Sauce, 198
Brownies, Applesauce, 200
Brussels Sprouts, Spruced-Up, 85
Buttermilk-Herb Dressing, 68
Butternut Squash & Apple Soup,
  102
Butter Piecrust, 160

C
Cabbage, Polish Sausage, Apples
  & Red, 121
cakes
  Chocolate-Applesauce Cake,
    164
  Kay Hollabaugh's Apple-Nut
    Cake, 163
  New York Apple-Bourbon
    Cake, 166, *167*
  Oatmeal-Apple Cupcakes,
    169
  Terri's Quick Apple Cake, 161
Calvados & Cider Soufflé, 190, *191*
Cameo, 220–21, *220*
canning apples, 206, 207, *207*
  Canned Applesauce, 209
  Canned Apple Slices, 208
  sterilizing jars/lids, 212
Caramel-Apple Puff Dumplings,
  203
Caramelized Apples, Phyllo Tarts
  with, 140, *141*
carrots
  Apple Muffins with Carrot &
    Coconut, 46, *47*
  Fragrant Lamb Stew, 126
celery

Triple Apple, Fruit & Veg
    Shake, 53
  Waldorf Salad, 73
cereal flakes
  Louise Salinger's Apple Pastry
    Squares, 156
Chapman, John, 181, 226
cheddar cheese
  Apple-Cheddar Crêpes, 29
  Apple-Cheese Spread, 63
  Apple-Corn Hotcakes, 32
  Apple Rarebit Supper, 105
  Baked Apples & Cheese, 106
  Cheese & Apple Tartlets, 152
  Cheese Pastry, 159
cheese. *See also* cheddar cheese;
  cream cheese
  Acorn Squash with Rice,
    Apple & Pecan Stuffing, 87
  Apple, Sausage & Cheese
    Strata, 90, *91*
  Apple & Parmesan Curl Salad,
    71
  Apple Frittata, 27
  Apple Pizza, 154
  low-fat options, 63
  Onion & Apple Samosas,
    60, *61*
Chenango Strawberry, 227
Chicken & Apple Gyros, 114, *115*
Chicken Salad, Curried, 77
Chicken with Apples, Turnips &
  Garlic, Roast, 116
Chicken with Sour Cream, Moroc-
  can Spiced, 113
chocolate/cocoa powder
  Applesauce Brownies, 200
  Chocolate-Applesauce Cake,
    164
  Sweet Little Bites, 204
Chutney, Apple, 108, *109*
Chutney, Rhubarb-Apple, 217
Ciderworks, 117
Cinnamon Soufflé, Apple-, 193
Cinnamon Squares, Apple-, 174,
  175
Cobbler, Apple-Apricot, 182, *183*
Cobbler, Barbara Mullin's Apple,
  181
Cocktails, Apple, 56
coconut/coconut milk
  Apple Muffins with Carrot &
    Coconut, 46, *47*

Baked Apple-Cranberry
    Oatmeal, 22
  Broiled Fish with Apple-
    Coconut Crust, 110
  Terri's Quick Apple Cake, 161
Codfish & Apple Curry, 111
Coffee Cake, Apple, 42, *43*
Coffee Can Bread, Barbara Mul-
  lin's, 41
conversion charts, metric, **233**
Cookies, Apple-Molasses, 172
Coriander & Cider Sauce, Sea
  Scallops with, 112
Corn Bread-Apple Stuffing, 94, *95*
Corn Hotcakes, Apple-, 32
Cortland, *147,* 221, *221*
Couscous Salad, Apple, Dried
  Fruit & Israeli, 74
Cox Orange Pippin, 227, *228*
cranberries
  Apple-Cinnamon Squares,
    174, *175*
  Apple-Cranberry Meringue
    Pie, 144, *145*
  Baked Apple-Cranberry
    Oatmeal, 22
  Fall Fruit Relish, 98
  Spicy Cranberry-Apple Relish,
    97
  Spruced-Up Brussels Sprouts,
    85
cream
  Apple & Sweet Potato Purée,
    83
  Apple Eggnog, 57
  Apple Fool, 194
  Baked Apples & Cheese, 106
  Calvados & Cider Soufflé,
    190, *191*
  Pork Chops with Apple Cream
    Sauce, 119
  Pumpkin-Apple Pie, 142
  Sherried Apple Crêpes, 187
  Waldorf Salad, 73
cream cheese
  Almond-Apple Streusel, 150
  Apple-Cheese Spread, 63
  Apple-Cream Cheese Tart,
    139
  Apple-Date Cream Cheese
    Spread, 49
  Apple Snacks, 62
  Apricot Cream Cheese
    Spread, 49

Honey Cream Cheese Spread, 49

Prosciutto Apple Wedges, 65

Simple Spice Frosting, 168

Crêpes, Apple-Cheddar, 29

Crêpes, Basic, 30

Crêpes, Breakfast Sausage, 28

Crêpes, Sherried Apple, 187

cucumber

 Chicken & Apple Gyros, 114, *115*

Curried Apple Meat Loaf, 129

Curried Chicken Salad, 77

Curried Ham & Apples, 124

Custard Sauce, English, 201

D

dates

 Apple & Date Squares, 173

 Apple-Date Cream Cheese Spread, 49

 Fall Fruit Relish, 98

Distillery Lane Ciderworks, 117

Doughnuts, Apple, 36, *37*

Dressing, Balsamic-Herb, 70

Dressing, Buttermilk-Herb, 70

Duchess of Oldenburg, 228

Dumplings, Apricot-Apple, 202

Dumplings, Caramel-Apple Puff, 203

E

eating, best apples for, 231

Eggnog, Apple, 57

eggs/egg whites/egg yolks

 Apple, Sausage & Cheese Strata, 90, *91*

 Apple-Cinnamon Soufflé, 193

 Apple Eggnog, 57

 Apple Frittata, 27

 Apple Puff Omelet, 24

 Apple Scramble, 26

 Apple Sponge Pudding, 196

 Avocado & Apple Composed Salad with Buttermilk-Herb Dressing, 68, *69*

 Baked Apples & Cheese, 106

 Basic Crêpes, 30

 Calvados & Cider Soufflé, 190, *191*

 English Custard Sauce, 201

 Meringue-Topped Baked Apples, 188

 Pumpkin-Apple Pie, 142

Sausage & Apple Omelet, 25

Vanilla Soufflé, 192

Empire, *147*

English Apple Crumble, 184

English Custard Sauce, 201

equipment, 90, 206

F

Fameuse, 228

Farro with Mushrooms, Onion & Apple, 75

fennel bulb/fennel fronds

 Apple, Pear & Beet Composed Salad with Balsamic-Herb Dressing, 70

 Apple, Sausage & Cheese Strata, 90, *91*

fish

 Broiled Fish with Apple-Coconut Crust, 110

 Codfish & Apple Curry, 111

 Tuna-Apple Tortilla Wraps, 107

 Tuna with Apple Chutney, Grilled, 108, *109*

Fortune, 221

Fragrant Lamb Stew, 126

Fresh Apple & Mango Smoothie, 54, *55*

Frittata, Apple, 27

Fritters, Apple-Ring, 34

Fritters, Grated-Apple, 33

Frosting, Simple Spice, 168

Frozen Apples, *210*, 211

Frozen Yogurt, Apple-Honey, 195

fruit, dried. *See also* raisins

 Apple, Dried Fruit & Israeli Couscous Salad, 74

 Apple-Apricot Cobbler, 182, *183*

Fruit & Veg Shake, Triple Apple, 53

Fruit Relish, Fall, 98

Fuji, 221, *221*

G

Gala, *147*, 221, *221*

garlic

 Butternut Squash & Apple Soup, 102

 Roast Chicken with Apples, Turnips & Garlic, 116

Gâteau, Pancake, 31

ginger, crystalized

Apple Chutney, 108, *109*

Gingerbread, Applesauce, 165

Ginger Gold, *147*, 221–22, *221*

Golden Delicious, 222, *222*

Granny Smith, 222, *222*

granola

 Granola, Applesauce & Yogurt Sundae, 23

 Maple Apple Crisp, 177

grapefruit

 Apple Marmalade, 215

Grated-Apple Fritters, 33

Ground-Lamb Kebabs with Apple-Mint Raita, 127

growers' cooperatives, 35

Gyros, Chicken & Apple, 114, *115*

H

Ham & Apples, Curried, 124

Hard Sauce, Breezy Hill, 198

Harvest Apple Pie, 134, *135*

health, 64, 105

heirloom varieties, 13–14, 226–230

herbs, fresh. *See also* mint, fresh

 Apple, Dried Fruit & Israeli Couscous Salad, 74

 Broiled Fish with Apple-Coconut Crust, 110

 Butternut Squash & Apple Soup, 102

 Farro with Mushrooms, Onion & Apple, 75

 Spruced-Up Brussels Sprouts, 85

 Zucchini & Apple Soup, 103

honey

 Apple-Honey Frozen Yogurt, 195

 Apple Sponge Pudding, 196

 Honey Cream Cheese Spread, 49

 Sweet Applesauce, 176

Honeycrisp, *147*, 222, *222*

Hotcakes, Apple-Corn, 32

I

Iced Apple Tea, 52

Idared, 222–23

J

jalapeño peppers

 Apple Chutney, 108, *109*

 Chicken & Apple Gyros, 114, *115*

Index

jam
>   Apricot Cream Cheese
>   Spread, 49
Jam, Joyse's Blackberry & Apple, 214
Jazz, 223, *223*
Jelly, Mint-Apple, 216
Jerseymac, 223
Johnny Appleseed, 181, 226
Johnny Appleseed Squares, 186
Jonagold, 223, *223*
Jonamac, 223
Jonathan, 228

K

Kay Hollabaugh's Apple-Nut Cake,
>   163
Kebabs, Apple, 89
Kebabs with Apple-Mint Raita,
>   Ground-Lamb, 127
kiwis
>   Avocado & Apple Composed
>   Salad with Buttermilk-Herb
>   Dressing, 68, *69*
>   Triple Apple, Fruit & Veg
>   Shake, 53
Kuchen, Apple, 168

L

Lady, 228, *228*
Lady Alice, 12
Lamb Kebabs with Apple-Mint
>   Raita, Ground-, 127
Lamb Stew, Fragrant, 126
Latkes, Potato & Apple, 96
leeks
>   Baked Apples & Cheese, 106
>   Spinach with Leek, Bacon &
>   Apple, 81
lemon/lemon juice/lemon zest
>   Apple, Dried Fruit & Israeli
>   Couscous Salad, 74
>   Apple Cider Sidecar, The, 56
>   Apple Marmalade, 215
>   Iced Apple Tea, 52
>   Prosciutto Apple Wedges, 65
>   Wassail, 57
Little Bites, Sweet, 204
Louise Salinger's Apple Meat Loaf,
>   130, *131*
Louise Salinger's Apple Pastry
>   Squares, 156
Louse Salinger's Apple Tea Bread,
>   39
low-fat baking, apples in, 154

M

Macoun, 223, *223*
Mango Smoothie, Fresh Apple
>   &, 54, *55*
maple syrup
>   Apple Maple Sauce, 34
>   Apple Sponge Pudding, 196
>   Maple Apple Crisp, 177
>   Maple-Sweet Potato Casse-
>   role, 84
Marmalade, Apple, 215
McIntosh, *147*, 224, *224*
Meat Loaf, Curried Apple, 129
Meat Loaf, Louise Salinger's
>   Apple, 130
Melrose, 224
Meringue-Topped Baked Apples,
>   188
metric conversion charts, 233
Miller, Rob, 117
mint, fresh
>   Ground-Lamb Kebabs with
>   Apple-Mint Raita, 127
>   Mint-Apple Jelly, 216
>   Waldorf Salad, 73
molasses
>   Apple-Molasses Cookies, 172
>   Applesauce Gingerbread,
>   165
Muffins, Applesauce, 45
Muffins, Bran-Applesauce, 44
Muffins with Carrot & Coconut,
>   Apple, 46, *47*
mushrooms
>   Farro with Mushrooms,
>   Onion & Apple, 75
>   Turkey Scaloppini with
>   Apple Cider and Mush-
>   rooms, 118
Mutsu/Crispin, 224, *224*

N

National Apple Month, 172
Newtown Pippin, 228
Northern Spy, 228, *228*
nuts. *See also* almonds; pecans;
>   walnuts
>   Apple & Parmesan Curl
>   Salad, 71
>   Apple-Nut Puff Tarts, 137
>   Fall Fruit Relish, 98
>   Johnny Appleseed Squares,
>   186
>   Kay Hollabaugh's Apple-Nut
>   Cake, 163

Maple Apple Crisp, 177
Microwave Apple Bread
>   Pudding, 197
Sweet Little Bites, 204

O

oatmeal/rolled oats
>   Almond-Apple Streusel, 150
>   Apple, Rhubarb & Strawberry
>   Streusel Pie, 148, *149*
>   Apple-Raisin Crunch, 185
>   Baked Apple-Cranberry
>   Oatmeal, 22
>   Maple Apple Crisp, 177
>   Oatmeal-Apple Cupcakes,
>   169
Omelet, Apple Puff, 24
Omelet, Sausage & Apple, 25
onions. *See also* scallions
>   Onion & Apple Samosas,
>   60, *61*
>   Rhubarb-Apple Chutney, 217
>   Sausage & Apple Stuffing, 93
oranges/orange juice/orange zest
>   Apple Butter, 213
>   Apple Marmalade, 215
>   Spicy Cranberry-Apple Relish,
>   97
orchards, 99, 162, 199

P

Pancake Gâteau, 31
Pancakes, Apple, 31
party, apple/cheese/wine, 62
Pastry, Cheese, 159
Pastry, Flaky, 157
Pastry, Short, 158
Patricia, 224
Paula Red, 224, *224*
pears
>   Apple, Pear & Beet Com-
>   posed Salad with Balsam-
>   ic-Herb Dressing, 70
>   Fall Fruit Relish, 98
pecans
>   Acorn Squash with Rice,
>   Apple & Pecan Stuffing, 87
>   Apple Coffee Cake, 42, *43*
>   Apple Crumb Pie, 146
>   Apple Kuchen, 168
>   Applesauce Brownies, 200
>   Barbara Mullin's Coffee Can
>   Bread, 41
>   Caramel-Apple Puff Dump-
>   lings, 203

peppers. *See* bell peppers; jala-
  peño peppers
phyllo dough
  Apple Strudel, 170, *171*
  Phyllo Tarts with Caramelized
    Apples, 140, *141*
pie, 212, 231
  Apple-Cranberry Meringue
    Pie, 144, *145*
  Apple Crumb Pie, 146
  Apple Envelope, 153
  Apple-Raspberry Pie, 143
  Beef & Apple Deep-Dish Pie,
    128
  Harvest Apple Pie, 134, *135*
  Pumpkin-Apple Pie, 142
Piecrust, Butter, 160
Piñata, 12
pineapple/pineapple juice
  Party Apple Punch, 56
  Triple Apple, Fruit & Veg
    Shake, 53
Pink Lady, 224, *225*
Pizza, Apple, 154
pork
  Curried Apple Meat Loaf, 129
  Curried Ham & Apples, 124
  Louise Salinger's Apple Meat
    Loaf, 130, *131*
  Pork Chops with Apple Cream
    Sauce, 119
  Pork Tenderloin Stuffed with
    Apples, 122, *123*
  Pork Tenderloin with Ap-
    ple-Shallot Sauce, 120
Porter, 229
potatoes. *See also* sweet potatoes
  Mashed Potatoes with Apples,
    82
  Potato & Apple Latkes, 96
  Potato-Apple Salad, 78, *79*
Pound Sweet, 229, *229*
Power, Patty, 117
preserves, making, 212–17
  about, 212
  recipes, 213–17
preserving apples, 206–7
  canning, 206, 207
  freezing, 206, 210, *210*
Prosciutto Apple Wedges, 65
Pudding, Apple Sponge, 196
Pudding, Microwave Apple Bread,
  197
puff pastry, frozen
  Apple-Nut Puff Tarts, 137

Caramel-Apple Puff Dump-
  lings, 203
Onion & Apple Samosas,
  60, *61*
Pumpkin-Apple Pie, 142
Punch, Party Apple, 56

R
raisins
  Apple-Cinnamon Squares, 174
  Apple Envelope, 153
  Apple-Nut Puff Tarts, 137
  Apple-Raisin Crunch, 185
  Apple Strudel, 170, *171*
  Codfish & Apple Curry, 111
  Curried Chicken Salad, 77
  Curried Ham & Apples, 124
  Rhubarb-Apple Chutney, 217
  Rice-Stuffed Apples, 88
Raita, Apple, 127
Raritan, 225
Raspberry Pie, Apple-, 143
Ratatouille, Apple, 86
Red Astrachan, 229, *229*
Red Cabbage, Polish Sausage,
  Apples &, 121
Red Delicious, 225, *225*
Relish, Fall Fruit, 98
Relish, Spicy Cranberry-Apple, 97
Rhode Island Greening, 229, *229*
Rhubarb & Strawberry Streusel
  Pie, Apple, 148, *149*
Rhubarb-Apple Chutney, 217
Rhubarb Slump, Apple-, 180
Rice, Apple & Pecan Stuffing,
  Acorn Squash with, 87
Rice-Stuffed Apples, 88
Roast Chicken with Apples,
  Turnips & Garlic, 116
Rolls, Applesauce & Whole-
  Wheat Yeast, 48
Rome Beauty, 225
Roxbury Russet, 229, *229*
Ryan, Elizabeth, 199

S
salad(s), 231
  Apple, Dried Fruit & Israeli
    Couscous Salad, 74
  Apple, Pear & Beet Com-
    posed Salad with Balsam-
    ic-Herb Dressing, 70
  Apple & Parmesan Curl Salad,
    71
  Apple-Tortellini Salad, 76

Avocado & Apple Composed
  Salad with Buttermilk-Herb
  Dressing, 68, *69*
Curried Chicken Salad, 77
Potato-Apple Salad, 78, *79*
Spinach-Apple Salad, 72
Waldorf Salad, 73
Samosas, Onion & Apple, 60, *61*
sauce(s), 231
  Apple Maple Sauce, 34
  Breezy Hill Hard Sauce, 198
  English Custard Sauce, 201
  White Chocolate-Vanilla
    Sauce, 151, *151*
sausage
  Apple, Sausage & Cheese
    Strata, 90, *91*
  Apple & Sausage Bundles, 59
  Black Bean Soup, 104
  Breakfast Sausage Crêpes, 28
  Polish Sausage, Apples & Red
    Cabbage, 121
  Sausage & Apple Omelet, 25
  Sausage & Apple Stuffing, 93
scallions
  Apple, Dried Fruit & Israeli
    Couscous Salad, 74
  Apple-Corn Hotcakes, 32
  Apple-Tortellini Salad, 76
  Sausage & Apple Omelet, 25
  Tuna-Apple Tortilla Wraps,
    107
Sea Scallops with Coriander &
  Cider Sauce, 112
Shake, Triple Apple, Fruit & Veg,
  53
Shallot Sauce, Pork Tenderloin
  with Apple-, 120
Sheepnose, 227
sherry
  Sherried Apple Crêpes, 187
  Wassail, 57
Short Pastry, 158
Simple Spice Frosting, 168
Slump, Apple-Rhubarb, 180
Smokehouse, 229
Smoothie, Fresh Apple & Mango,
  54, *55*
snacks
  Apple Snacks, 62
  breakfast/after-school, 26
Snow, 228
Sops of Wine, 229
Sorbet, Apple, 194
Soufflé, Apple-Cinnamon, 193

Soufflé, Calvados & Cider, 190, *191*
Soufflé, Vanilla, 192
Soup, Black Bean, 104
Soup, Butternut Squash & Apple, 102
Soup, Zucchini & Apple, 103
sour cream
    Apple & Sweet Potato Purée, 83
    Apple Coffee Cake, 42, *43*
    Apple Crumb Pie, 146
    Apple Pancakes, 31
    Curried Chicken Salad, 77
    Mashed Potatoes with Apples, 82
    Moroccan Spiced Chicken with Sour Cream, 113
    Terri's Quick Apple Cake, 161
sparkling cider/wine
    Party Apple Punch, 56
spinach
    Apple-Tortellini Salad, 76
    Spinach-Apple Salad, 72
    Spinach with Leek, Bacon & Apple, 81
    Triple Apple, Fruit & Veg Shake, 53
Spruced-Up Brussels Sprouts, 85
Squash & Apple Soup, Butternut, 102
Squash with Rice, Apple & Pecan Stuffing, Acorn, 87
Stayman, 225
Strata, Apple, Sausage & Cheese, 90, *91*
strawberries
    Apple, Rhubarb & Strawberry Streusel Pie, 148, *149*
    Apple-Tortellini Salad, 76
    Fresh Apple & Mango Smoothie, 54, *55*
Streusel, Almond-Apple, 150
Strudel, Apple, 170, *171*
Stuffed Apples, Whole, 211
stuffing
    Apple & Red Bell Pepper Stuffing Balls, 92
    Corn Bread-Apple Stuffing, 94, *95*
    Sausage & Apple Stuffing, 93
Summer Rambo, 230
Sundae, Granola, Applesauce & Yogurt, 23

Sweetango, 12–13
Sweet Applesauce, 176
sweetened condensed milk
    Johnny Appleseed Squares, 186
Sweet Little Bites, 204
sweet potatoes
    Apple & Sweet Potato Purée, 83
    Maple-Sweet Potato Casserole, 84

T
tarts/tartlets
    Apple-Cream Cheese Tart, 139
    Apple-Nut Puff Tarts, 137
    Cheese & Apple Tartlets, 152
    French Apple Tart, 136
    Phyllo Tarts with Caramelized Apples, 140, *141*
Tea, Iced Apple, 52
Terri's Quick Apple Cake, 161
Tolman Sweet, 230
tomatoes
    Avocado & Apple Composed Salad with Buttermilk-Herb Dressing, 68, *69*
Tompkins King, 230
Tortellini Salad, 76
Tortilla Wraps, Tuna-Apple, 107
Tuna with Apple Chutney, Grilled, 108, *109*
turkey
    Louise Salinger's Apple Meat Loaf, 130, *131*
    Turkey Scaloppini with Apple Cider and Mushrooms, 118
Turnips & Garlic, Roast Chicken with Apples, 116
Turnovers, Apple, 155
Twenty Ounce, 230
Two Simple Apple Desserts, 194

U
Unsweetened Applesauce, 80, *80*

V
Vanilla Soufflé, 192

W
Waldorf Salad, 73
walnuts
    Apple & Date Squares, 173

Apple Pizza, 154
Applesauce & Whole-Wheat Yeast Rolls, 48
Baked Apple-Cranberry Oatmeal, 22
Farro with Mushrooms, Onion & Apple, 75
Louse Salinger's Apple Tea Bread, 39
New York Apple-Bourbon Cake, 166, *167*
Spinach-Apple Salad, 72
Waldorf Salad, 73
Whole-Wheat & Nut Quick Bread, 40
Wassail, 57
Wealthy, 230
Westfield Seek-No-Further, 230, *230*
White Chocolate-Vanilla Sauce, 151, *151*
Whole-Wheat & Nut Quick Bread, 40
Whole-Wheat Yeast Rolls, Applesauce &, 48
Winesap, 225, *225*
Winter Banana, 230, *230*
Wolf River, 230
Wraps, Tuna-Apple Tortilla, 107

Y
yogurt
    Apple-Honey Frozen Yogurt, 195
    Apple Pancakes, 31
    Apple Raita, 127
    Chicken & Apple Gyros, 114, *115*
    Curried Apple Meat Loaf, 129
    Fresh Apple & Mango Smoothie, 54, *55*
    Granola, Applesauce & Yogurt Sundae, 23
    Spinach-Apple Salad, 72
York Imperial, 226

Z
Zestar! 13
zucchini
    Apple Ratatouille, 86
    Zucchini & Apple Soup, 103